Classic Fifties Cars

CRESTLINE

First published in 2006 by MBI Publishing Company

Fifties Fins © Dennis David, 2001
Fifties American Cars © Mike Mueller, 1994

ISBN13: 978-0-7603-2710-4
ISBN10: 0-7603-2710-6

Printed in China

On the cover: Like Chevrolet's 1957 Bel Air, Ford's early Thunderbirds are easily recognized today be even the most casual observers. Truncated two-seat renditions of Ford's mainline 1955 and 1956 models, the T-bird grew slightly in 1957 thanks to a longer tail section wearing more pronounced fins.

On page 7: DeSoto's rear quarter was a perfect blend of trim work that in later years would prove to be a hit at any car show. A triple taillight theme set off by angular lines and gold anodized trim set the top-of-the-line Adventurer convertible apart from the competition. Despite its wonderful style and solid reputation, DeSoto was only a few short years away from its ultimate demise.

On the title page: Ford Motor Company fans who thought the 1952-1954 Lincolns were hot luxury bombs had another coming once Chrysler introduced its letter-series models in 1955. With a 300hp hemi-head V-8 beneath the hood, the lavish 1955 C-300 emerged as Detroit's most powerful production car, and could easily run with anything on the road. An exciting restyle in 1957 fit the equally exciting 300C to a tee.

On the back cover: Oldsmobile's top-of-the-line offering for 1956 was the Series 98 Starfire convertible. At $3,380, it was expensive, but came with Oldsmobile's 3240inch Rocket V-8 that was rated at 340 horsepower. The Rocket engine was used for many racing endeavors, and famed driver Lee Petty would set a new record t Daytona in the flying mile at 144 miles per hour driving an Oldsmobile. The use of two-tone paint schemes and a unique taillight treatment made for an attractive package. Oldsmobile made only 8,581 Starfire convertibles for 1956; this example is finished in Black and Alcan White.

CONTENTS

FIFTIES
American Cars

Mike Mueller

Acknowledgments

Creating this short-winded epic wouldn't have been at all possible without the patience, cooperation, and, above all, hospitality of the many proud car collectors whose classic fifties machines appear on these pages. Although the author would love to thank each and every one personally, he is well aware that listing their names here would require far less effort. But seriously, thanks so much everyone for your kindness. In basic order of appearance, the lucky owners are:

Larry Young, Port Charlotte, Florida, 1955, 1956, and 1957 Chevrolets; Bob Dykstra, Ageless Autos, Zeeland, Michigan, 1950 Ford; Gerald Schantz, Ormond Beach, Florida, 1957 Cadillac Eldorado Brougham; Bill and Barbara Jacobsen, Silver Dollar Classic Cars, Odessa, Florida, 1959 Chevrolet Impala; Jim and Betty Pardo, Naples, Florida, 1951 Buick Special; Larry Young, Port Charlotte, Florida, 1955 Chevrolet Bel Air convertible; Wilton and Terry Davis, Valrico, Florida, 1955 Ford Victoria; Ronald Layton, Sparta, New Jersey, 1955 Mercury Montclair Sun Valley; Mike Bloore, Lutz, Florida, 1957 Ford Skyliner Retractable; Don and Pat Petrus, Winter Haven, Florida, 1957 Ford Thunderbird; Walter and Marion Gutowski, Lakeland, Florida, 1958 Buick Limited convertible; Bill Henefelt, Clearwater, Florida, 1959 Cadillac Series 62 convertible; Charles and Virginia Stoneking, Winter Haven, Florida, 1959 Edsel Ranger; Art and June Ubbens, Lake Wales, Florida, 1955 Plymouth Belvedere; Robert and Mary McVeigh, Lake Park, Florida, 1959 Pontiac Catalina convertible; John Young, Mulberry, Florida, 1954 Corvette; Edwin Hobart, Naples, Florida, 1954 Kaiser Darrin; Rich Miller, Clearwater, Florida, 1957 Chevrolet Bel Air convertible; George Shelley, Pompano Beach, Florida, 1957 Chrysler 300C; Floyd Garrett, Fernandina Beach, Florida, 1957 Ford Fairlane; Don McCullen, Gainesville, Florida, 1957 Studebaker Golden Hawk; Marvin and Joan Hughes, Ocala, Florida, 1957 Dodge Coronet D500 convertible; Gary Ogeltree, Fayetteville, Georgia, 1958 Plymouth Fury; Doug West, Preston, Idaho, 1959 DeSoto Adventurer; Era Harvey, Leesburg, Florida, 1950 Skorpion, 1951

Crosley, and 1958 King Midget; Gene Schild, Des Plaines, Illinois, 1953 Packard Caribbean; Rick Lay, Athens, Tennessee, 1953 Kaiser Dragon; Dave Horton, Lakeland, Florida, 1954 Willys Aero Lark; Harry Fry, Lake Wales, Florida, 1951 Crosley Farm-O-Road; George and Katherine Baumann, Davie, Florida, 1954 Hudson Hornet; Marc Harr, Ormond Beach, Florida, 1955 Packard Clipper; Larry and Vickie Gehm, Melbourne, Florida, 1954 Ford Customline Ranch Wagon; Erol and Susan Tuzcu, Del Ray Beach, Florida, 1957 Chevrolet Nomad; Al Whitcombe, Ambler, Pennsylvania, 1956 Ford F100 pickup; Halderman Ford, Kutztown, Pennsylvania, 1991 Ford F150 XLT 4x4; Bob and Linda Ogle, Champaign, Illinois, 1956 Chevrolet Cameo Carrier pickup; Bob and Debbie Higgins, Davie, Florida, 1957 Chevrolet 3100 pickup; Dan Topping, Tifton, Georgia, 1957 Dodge Sweptside D100 pickup; Ron Fisher, Indianapolis, Indiana, 1957 Ford Ranchero; Doug Stapleton, Bradenton, Florida, 1959 Chevrolet El Camino; Stuart Echolls, Lakeland, Florida, 1955 Dodge Royal; James Wienke, Homer, Illinois, 1955 Ford Crown Victoria; Dan Newcombe of Golden Classics, Safety Harbor, Florida, 1958 Dodge Coronet; Dwight and Mabel Caler, Bradenton, Florida, 1950 Studebaker Champion; William Stead, Lake Mary, Florida, 1953 Henry J; and Gene Jr., Sherri, and Christie DeBlasio, Plantation Florida, 1955 Chevrolet Nomad.

Introduction

The Decade That Just Keeps Rolling On

For many among us it was the longest ten years in history, recorded or otherwise. By definition it was simply another decade, one that began on January 1, 1950, then ended on December 31, 1959. Or did it? Just as time marches on, so too have the fifties, those Fabulous Fifties, right on through the sixties, seventies, eighties, and into the nineties. Sure, memories tend to linger—they wouldn't be memories if they didn't. But for whatever reasons, remembrances of the fifties have not only refused to fade from the American consciousness, they have, in many cases, grown larger than life at a rate unmatched by virtually any other time period.

Dissecting this phenomenon is not something done lightly, nor is it the goal of this humble 96-page offering. Pulitzer Prize-winning journalist David Halberstam needed nearly 750 pages to do the job, and nowhere within his latest, perhaps heaviest epic—simply and appropriately titled "The Fifties"—can readers find a discussion of what made Chevy's "Hot One" so hot, a detailed description of Virgil Exner's "100 Million Dollar Look," or any reference whatsoever to "dagmars." This much lighter publication, on the other hand, is not about McCarthyism, Cold War sabre-rattling, Marilyn Monroe's moles, or Brooklyn's Dodgers moving west. As the title you passed a few pages back might indicate, this is a book about cars, particularly the fabulous cars of the Fabulous Fifties.

Like the decade itself, who can forget all those wonderful machines, many of which have grown in nostalgic prominence right along with the times

Left
Find someone who doesn't recognize the classic Chevy triumvirate, and you're probably not on this planet. Called the "Hot One" for its newfound overhead-valve V-8 performance, the 1955 Chevrolet Bel Air (front)

helped change the way buyers in the low-priced field looked at daily transportation. Chevy's Hot One grew even hotter in 1956 (middle), thanks to an optional 225hp V-8, then became everyone's nostalgic favorite in 1957 (back).

Detroit's first major styling change of the postwar era involved dumping the ever-present pontoon fenders common to all cars of the thirties and forties. Ford's all-new postwar look, introduced in 1949, was easily the cleanest of the fresh "slabside" style. That same modern bodyshell returned for 1950 (shown here) with few changes, then reappeared again in similar fashion for 1951.

from which they sprang? Some, such as modern cult favorites like the 1957 Chevy and 1957 Thunderbird, are easily recalled with enthusiasm by even the most casual observer. Others, like Studebaker's 1953 "Loewy coupe," the 1954 Hudson Hornet, and custom-bodied Buick Skylarks of 1953–1954, are far less renowned among the armchair set but are still deserving of every bit as much respect as their more publicized contemporaries. The fifties represented a veritable cornucopia of automotive delights—and disappointments. What other decade offered such disparate creations as the lavish Cadillac Eldorado Brougham and the impish Crosley Hot Shot? Classics, milestones, failures, and flops, they

SEE THE SCENERY THROUGH THE ROOF—see traffic lights easily—yet tinted transparent top protects against heat, wind, glare.

Presenting The Sun Valley—America's First Transparent-Top Car

You've seen pictures of dream cars of tomorrow. But you couldn't buy them. Now, Mercury presents America's first transparent top car to be put into regular production!

The entire front half of the roof is tinted Plexiglas. You have a wonderful sensation of driving with no top at all—but with the wind and weather protection of a sedan.

And with the great new 161-horsepower Mercury V-8 engine that makes any driving easy—the unique Sun Valley is bound to be 1954's most exciting car. See it today!

MERCURY DIVISION · FORD MOTOR COMPANY

NEW 1954
MERCURY

A new kind of power that makes *any* driving easy

---

were all present and accounted for in spades during the fifties.

Why? Various reasons, certainly, but the most prominent one involves the plain fact that this country's so-called "baby boom" wasn't the only explosion heard during the fifties. While U.S. military men fresh from World War II's battle fronts busily populated suburban America by doing their duty at home, Yankee industry was experiencing a growth cycle of its own, both upward and outward. Lessons learned during the war's frenzied production days were not lost as peacetime practices resumed, and it was undoubtedly the auto industry that gained the most from its education. After turning out tanks, planes, and guns at astronomical rates, supplying civilian transportation for Mainstreet U.S.A. was a piece of cake—at least as far as quantity was concerned.

By 1946, new-car-starved Americans were beating down Detroit's doors, but all Detroit could do at first was roll out a steady supply of prewar rehashes. New only by label, 1946 cars looked an awful lot like the last models built before wartime restrictions shut down automotive production early in

---

See-through plastic roof sections were nothing new in 1954; exotic showcars had appeared in previous years sporting transparent tops. But only Ford Motor Company tried the practice in regular production. Both Mercury's

Sun Valley and Ford's Skyliner featured tinted plexiglass instead of steel over the front seat. Mercury tried the trick one more time in 1955; Ford built its Skyliner into 1956.

Above
In 1993, Chevrolet celebrated four decades of building "America's only sports car" by rolling out a fortieth anniversary model (right), offered in one shade only, Ruby Red Metallic. When introduced in 1953, Chevy's fiberglass two-seater also came in only one shade, Polo White, and was powered by a six-cylinder engine backed by a Powerglide automatic transmission.

Right
Chevrolet's Corvette was entering its third year when Ford responded with a four-wheel legend of its own, the Thunderbird. Similar in size and also seating only two, the 1955 Thunderbird was a bird of a very different feather, offering buyers both class and comfort. Dearborn called this new style "personal luxury." After returning in 1956 and 1957, the T-bird became a little less personal when two more seats were added for 1958.

IMPERIAL

THIS MAN COULDN'T HAVE DONE BETTER . . . AND HE KNOWS IT!

He steps to the curb, dynamic and confident. He's a man who seems big, although after he has driven away you don't especially remember whether he was or not.

What you do remember is the strength of his personality, the way people went out of their way to speak to him. And the glances of approval he got when his car arrived.

It could only be one car — an Imperial. The car and the man are perfect complements — the man of substance and the most impressive car on the road today.

Imperial bespeaks power, leadership and good taste. It is designed for the man who is successful and doesn't have to prove it . . . for the man who doesn't seek prestige because he already has it.

Looking at an Imperial, riding in it, driving it . . . these things change your concept of fine car ownership. But you need more than money. Genuine good taste is a part of the purchase price. This is why the trend today, among the most critical and the most discriminating motorists in America, is definitely to Imperial.

Why not ask your Chrysler dealer for an appointment? He'll be glad to arrange one at your convenience.

THE FINEST CAR AMERICA HAS YET PRODUCED

Chrysler Corporation set off the Imperial models as a separate line beginning in 1955, the year stylist Virgil Exner put all Chrysler's divisions on Detroit's cutting edge as far as looks were concerned. One of the fifties true classics, the 1955 Imperial was easily spotted thanks to its "gunsight" taillights.

Cadillac's Eldorado Brougham of 1957 was more a palace on wheels than a car. Along with every known type of power accessory, Eldorado Brougham features also included perfume bottles, cigarette dispensers, and a mini-bar in the glove box. Throw in a stainless-steel roof, four-wheel air suspension and a 300hp 365ci V-8 fed by twin four-barrel carburetors and it was little wonder this luxury showboat cost $13,000.

1942. Promises of all-new postwar automobiles had been plentiful as World War II wound down, but since initial peacetime demand easily outstripped supply, Detroit's most prominent movers and shakers were able to take what some witnesses perceived as their own sweet time fulfilling those promises.

As a newcomer starting from scratch, Kaiser-Frazer couldn't help being Detroit's first automaker to offer totally fresh postwar cars, introduced in October 1946 as 1947 models. Another independent, Studebaker, also jumped on the totally new bandwagon in 1947. The South Bend, Indiana, automaker's flexibility came not from newness (Studebaker had been in the transportation business for nearly 100 years) but from its relative small size compared to Detroit's giants.

Gadgetry abounded in the fifties, especially from Chrysler, which offered swivel bucket seats, clocks in steering wheel hubs, and pushbutton transmissions. These buttons control Chrysler's excellent three-speed Torqueflite automatic in a 1957 300C convertible, one of the fifties most powerful cruisers.

Further proving that independents had to try harder than the heavily entrenched "Big Three," Hudson was next out with a thoroughly modern postwar model, featuring its innovative "step-down" unit-body chassis for 1948. Featuring widely spaced perimeter frame rails, Hudson's intriguing stepdown design meant the passenger compartment floor could be placed low between those rails, which in turn made for a lower, sleeker bodyshell. And like those eye-catching Kaisers and Frazers of 1947, the new 1948 Hudson featured full "slabside," modern styling—no more archaic pontoon fenders.

Among Detroit's ruling triumvirate—General Motors, Ford Motor Company, and Chrysler Corporation—it was GM that jumped out of the postwar starting blocks first, introducing a restyled Cadillac in 1948. Revamped Buicks, Oldsmobiles, Pontiacs, and Chevrolets followed in 1949, a watershed year for the modern postwar market as Ford and Chrysler also entered the fray. By 1950, the redesigned line-up was complete, and the games began.

Even though it had introduced the same basic platform in 1949, Ford greeted customers the following year with the slogan "50 ways new for 1950." If you were skeptical, you could count all 50 ways spread out right there across two pages in *Life* magazine. New, newer, newest—just when you'd thought you'd seen it all, along came another automaker's claim to top everything that had come before. Competitive pressures to build the biggest, best, most beautiful cars grew exponentially as the decade progressed, leading to rapid, welcomed, technological development, as well as some not-so-welcome design extremes. But either way, forward or backward, the American auto industry's

Chrysler Corporation, thanks to stylist Virgil Exner's touch, was head and shoulders above the rest in the tailfin department. By 1959, few cars could match the towering fins on Chryslers, DeSotos, Plymouths, and Dodges. But if there was one car that was the king of the fin era, it was the 1959 Cadillac.

progress during the fifties was anything but dull.

In 1950, Ford was still dedicated to its antiquated, valve-in-block "flathead" V-8, Chrysler Corporation was experimenting with various "semi-automatic" transmissions that shifted on their own at speed but still required a clutch for starting, and Cadillac taillights were topped by humble bulges modeled after the twin tailfins of Lockheed's P-38 Lightning fighter plane. By 1959, modern, high-revving overhead-valve V-8s had all but vanquished the old, clunky flatheads; Chrysler's bulletproof three-speed Torqueflite automatic represented state-of-the-art transmission fare; and Cadillac tailfins were boldly soaring to heights few tailfins had ever achieved.

In 1950, it seemed most cars were green, beige, or black, with maybe a red or yellow one thrown in now and again to spice things up for the truly adventurous car buyer. Five years later, a solid crimson finish was almost ho-hum in comparison to the seemingly countless two-tone combinations available. Packard and Studebaker even offered triple-tone paint schemes. And if that wasn't enough, GM customers in 1958 were left wondering if chrome had become an exterior color choice.

In 1950, Dodge, Plymouth, and DeSoto models featured what was known as three-box styling—stacked high in the middle, short, squat, and squared off at both ends—in Chrysler Corporation's best conservative tradition. Nine years later, Pontiac was leading GM towards a totally different design horizon with its long and low 1959 "Wide Track" models, cars that were illegal in some states that specified maximum body widths.

A scant four years earlier, Pontiac had begun a transformation from a stuffy, stoic company that sold cars grandpa drove to builders of true excitement. Corporate cousin Chevrolet had led the way, making a seemingly overnight transformation in 1955 by superseding its old, reliable "Stovebolt six" image with modern overhead-valve V-8 power. Simply labeled the "Hot One," the redesigned 1955 Chevy with its optional 265ci overhead-valve (ohv) V-8 almost single-handedly changed the way Americans looked at their daily transportation. A triple-digit top end had never come this cheap, and actually hadn't come much at all before GM started spreading its proven engineering wealth around to its less prestigious divisions. Once reserved only for high-brow Cadillac and Oldsmobile buyers, truly hot, high-winding OHV V-8 performance made an instant impact in the low-priced field. Muscle for the masses? You betcha. Just like that, Detroit had itself a horsepower race.

Competition of another color helped homogenize the American automaking scene as the fifties rolled on. Not that the composition of the Big Three was ever in any flux, but by 1959 GM, Ford, and Chrysler officials had next to no one to worry about other than themselves. Most independent rivals had all but fallen by the wayside, basically because they didn't have the cash to keep up with their rapidly retooling rivals.

Kaiser was a promising prospect in the years immediately following World War II, but it left the American market in 1955, taking Willys with it. Once proud, independent, pillars of the prewar automaking community, Packard and Studebaker merged in 1954 to pool their shrinking resources, then slowly faded away in the sixties. Another 1954 merger brought old stalwarts Hudson and Nash together under the American Motors banner.

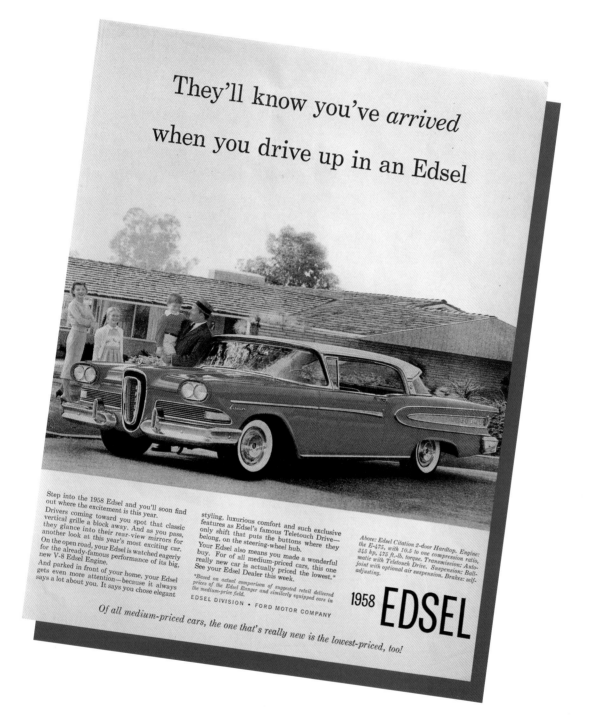

They'll know you've *arrived* when you drive up in an Edsel

Step into the 1958 Edsel and you'll soon find out where the excitement is this year. Drivers coming toward you spot that classic vertical grille a block away. And as you pass, they glance into their rear-view mirrors for another look at this year's most exciting car. On the open road, your Edsel is watched eagerly for the already-famous performance of its big, new V-8 Edsel Engine.

And parked in front of your home, your Edsel gets even more attention—because it always says a lot about you. It says you chose elegant styling, luxurious comfort and such exclusive features as Edsel's famous Teletouch Drive—only shift that puts the buttons where they belong, on the steering-wheel hub.

Your Edsel also means you made a wonderful buy. For of all medium-priced cars, this one really new car is actually priced the lowest. See your Edsel Dealer this week.

Based on actual comparison of suggested retail delivered prices of the Edsel Ranger and similarly equipped cars in the medium-price field.

EDSEL DIVISION • FORD MOTOR COMPANY

Above: Edsel Citation 2-door Hardtop. Engine: the E-475, with 10.5 to one compression ratio. 345 hp, 475 ft.-lb. torque. Transmission: Automatic with Teletouch Drive. Suspension: Ball-joint with optional air suspension. Brakes: self-adjusting.

1958 **EDSEL**

Of all medium-priced cars, the one that's really new is the lowest-priced, too!

Even though it sold reasonably well in a recession-racked year, Ford Motor Company's Edsel became the butt of countless jokes shortly after its 1958 debut. Falling well short of Dearborn's sales goal for its new mid-priced division, Edsel returned in 1959, then made one last feeble appearance the following year before exiting stage right.

In 1958, the Rambler marque supplanted the Hudson and Nash names, and the corporation managed to survive the fifties by joining the newly formed compact car ranks.

While independent automakers were struggling for their very survival in the fifties, Detroit's entrenched powers were busy overwhelming their customers with a wide array of futuristic features, clever convenience options, and dazzling design tricks. Automakers in the fifties were no strangers to gadgetry and gizmos. Headlights automatically dimmed when oncoming lights appeared, transparent speedometers mounted atop dashboards illuminated thanks to sunlight shining in through the windshield, and convertible tops went up by themselves with the first drop of rain on a fender. Ford offered a car with a tan-through plexiglass top and another that was both a hardtop and a convertible at the same time. Pushbutton transmissions, swivel bucket seats, "spinner" hubcaps, "signal tower" taillights—the list of head-turning, eye-catching, imagination-expanding, widgets and wonderments is almost endless.

Many features taken for granted just a half a decade later first appeared in the fifties. Originally, an extremely high-priced, somewhat complicated doodad, air conditioning began appearing on various options lists midway through the fifties, while four-barrel carburetors quickly became the only way to fly in the performance field.

New concepts introduced in the fifties also included an honest-to-goodness Yankee entry into the European-dominated sports car field and an all-American four-wheel ideal known as "personal luxury." The former, Chevrolet's fabled Corvette, was first on the scene in 1953 and helped inspire

the latter, Ford's lovable two-seat Thunderbird, two years later. If only Detroit could create such timeless automotive legends so easily today.

But of course not everything that rolled off a production line in the fifties was the stuff of legends. Quality control was not always up to snuff, especially early in the decade, and many models—too many actually—were certified rust magnets. At the opposite end of the decade, Detroit's move into the truly large-car field may have been inspired by the times but ended up proving that bigger isn't always better. Consequently, buyers also began to understand what "less is more" actually meant as fins skyrocketed and more and more chrome was piled on. Without a doubt, 1958 represented chrome-plating's blinding zenith, while tailfins hit their peak in 1959 before being unceremoniously clipped the following year.

Nineteen-fifty-eight also marked the debut of the one car that has come to symbolize—unjustly or not—much of what was wrong with fifties American automobiles. A victim of both a national recession as well as changing attitudes concerning styling, Ford Motor Company's Edsel quickly became the butt of jokes that are still heard today, though biting attack has long since been replaced with nostalgic amusement.

Time certainly does tend to heal all wounds, and such has been the case as far as the fifties are concerned. Most bad memories—an unpopular police action in Korea, segregation in the South, stifled sexuality everywhere (except maybe in Hollywood)—have generally been swept under the rug. Sure, there was much, much more to the fifties story than poodle skirts and ducktails, but we'll let Mr. Halberstam handle those chapters.

Even Chevrolet head stylist Claire MacKichan later admitted his men stepped a bit too far beyond sensibilities when they redesigned the Chevy for 1959. Had those flat fins stood up in typical fashion, they would have topped even corporate cousin Cadillac's high-flying appendages. Combined with a very busy grille and chrome-encrusted front end, the 1959 Chevrolet's "Manta Ray stern," as *Mechanix Illustrated's* Tom McCahill called it, inspired rival designers to describe the car as a "Martian Ground Chariot."

As far as many baby boomers today are concerned, the fifties represented a simpler time when rock 'n roll was king, Ward Cleaver was the mother of all fathers, and there was nothing cooler than an Olds Rocket 88. It was a time when kids actually pedaled around proudly with Mickey Mantle's rookie card clothespinned to their bicycle spokes, an entire family could easily afford an afternoon trip to the ballpark to see their favorite team play (on grass), and Duesenbergs were occasionally found on used car lots. And as long as nostalgia remains a great American pastime, the fifties—like Elvis himself—will never die, especially with all these wonderful reminders rolling around to keep the memories alive.

Chapter 1

Sign Posts and Mile Markers

History Makers; Good, Bad Or Ugly

Telling the tale of this country's great cars of the fifties is not something easily done in a quick read, considering everything that happened during the decade. So much history, so few years. Ten to be exact. But if you compare 1950 to 1959, it might well have been a hundred. Anyway you looked at it, from a technological perspective or with an eye towards tastes and trendiness, the transformation of the American automobile during the fifties had a lot in common with the progression of night into day.

With so much to talk about, good or bad, where do you begin? Although technology's march through the fifties cannot be overlooked, if you chose to start at the beginning, there's one major automotive attraction that rapidly grew in promi-nence right along with the years—style. No, style wasn't invented in the fifties, nor were earlier decades devoid of it. But beginning just before 1950, Detroit seemingly suddenly learned that heavy doses of style appeared to be just what the doctor ordered to keep the competition away. Whether style meant the way a car looked, or how sporty it felt, or how many gadgets it carried didn't matter. Style was style, and the fifties were soon full of it.

Before World War II, so many cars looked an awful lot like so many others. Basic transportation was the priority, with four-wheeled style and status existing only for the lucky few. After the war, car-makers quickly learned what it took to turn heads, and practical durability wasn't the answer.

Left
Seemingly overshadowed by its thoroughly modern running mates among General Motors early-fifties lineup, Buick stuck with its tried and true straight-eight powerplant while Cadillac and Oldsmobile were impressing buyers with overhead-valve V-8s. Buick styling, however, was, in keeping with fifties trends, never dull, as this 1951 Special's "waterfall" grill and ever-present "ventiports" (portholes to the casual observer) on the fender attest.

Although Ford's 1951 Victoria hardtop kept pace with one of Detroit's hottest styling trends—the pillarless coupe design—it was still powered by Dearborn's aging "flathead" V-8, first offered in 1932. Ford's first modern overhead-valve V-8, the so-called "Y-block," didn't arrive until 1954.

An all-new, modern look was the key to luring buyers hungry for truly modern cars into showrooms. Pontoon fenders—the antiquated calling cards of the thirties and forties—were out, smooth, "slabside" bodies were in. Newcomer Kaiser-Frazer stepped out first with slabside styling in late 1946, followed almost immediately by Studebaker, Cadillac in 1948, and Ford in 1949. While GM cars and Studebakers still carried vestiges of the old pontoon style (in the rear) into the fifties, Ford's styling crew held nothing back, resulting in probably the cleanest of the early slabside designs, a look that carried over from 1950 to 1951.

While bodysides were being transformed into solid walls of steel, various dress-up tactics were also developing at the tail. Under the direction of styling guru Harley Earl, GM's designers had in 1948 added two small fins above the Cadillac's taillights, kicking off what is easily the best-known fifties styling craze. Soon all of Detroit was playing with fins, noticeable or not. Fins first sprouted on Fords in 1952, but were always relatively downplayed, while Chrysler Corporation's took off in 1957, soaring to all-new heights by 1959. Thunderbird fins in 1957 were canted, Kaiser-Willys' fins faced the wrong way, and Chevrolet tried horizontal ones in 1959. Without a doubt, the best remembered fins of the fifties were those of the 1959 Cadillac, suitably so since it was the marque that started it all in the first place.

Another stylish trend that flourished in the fifties involved the newly developed hardtop bodystyle, or convertible coupe as it was sometimes known. Chrysler had toyed with the idea in 1947, creating an attractive, airy roofline by simply attaching a steel hardtop to a Town & Country

While Chevrolet always seems to hog all the credit for being the star of the 1955 model year, the new Fords that year were certainly no slouches. Flagship of Dearborn's 1955 model lines was the Crown Victoria, the creative product of designer L. David Ash. A "Crown Vic" was easily recognized by the forward-raked chrome band that wrapped over the roof. Ford tried this trick again in 1956.

convertible body, effectively deleting the "B-pillar," or "post" common to more mundane sedans. Only seven Chrysler prototypes were built, leaving credit for actually producing a regular-production hardtop to Cadillac, which it did in 1949, rolling out the Coupe DeVille.

Typically, rival variations on the hardtop theme quickly followed. Chrysler tried it again, this time successfully, with the Town & Country in 1950, followed by Ford's Victoria in 1951, Packard that same year, and Lincoln and Mercury in 1952. Frazer even offered an intriguing four-door hardtop in 1951, although it wasn't a full hardtop in the true sense in that this somewhat peculiar Manhattan model still incorporated an odd framed window in the area where a sedan's B-pillar would have resided. More conventional four-door hardtops would soon appear from the

Always seemingly one step behind Chevrolet in the fifties, Ford also put on a new face in 1955, although history has tended to overlook that fact. Two-tone paint schemes—pleasing, contrasting, or outright clashing—came into their own that year as most automakers began offering long lists of multiple color combinations.

Big Three, and four-door hardtop station wagons would eventually come along as well, first from American Motors in 1956, then from Buick, Oldsmobile, and Mercury the following year.

Always seemingly leading the way in one fashion or another, GM also established yet another styling trend in the fifties, this one involving the windshield. Advances in glass production technology, permitted a more stylish wraparound windshield, first tried by Cadillac on its 1953 Motorama dream car, the Eldorado convertible. Unlike conventional, basically flat windshields, GM's wraparound front glass did just that; it wrapped around at the corners, making for a more open, airy feel up front, much like the hardtop roofline had done at the sides. There was a trade-off, however. Warping the windshield around the corners created a "dogleg," an obtrusive projection at the top of the door opening's leading edge required to mount the wrapped glass' frame. Many a driver in the fifties would quickly learn what those doglegs did to your knees if you weren't careful while entering or exiting, and this bruising problem wouldn't be completely solved until the sixties.

Before 1955, Chevrolets were yeoman machines powered by frugal six-cylinders carrying equally frugal price tags. Although typically dull, they were still Detroit's perennial sales leader. But Chevrolet upset the low-priced field completely in 1955 with the legendary "Hot One," a car with an all-new look as well as Chevy's first modern OHV V-8.

Also incorporating wraparound front glass was Oldsmobile's lavish Fiesta convertible, another 1953 Motorama showcar that, like the Eldorado, rolled right off the show circuit into limited production. Two other high-profile, custom-built, top-less automobiles, Buick's Skylark and Chevrolet's fiberglass-bodied Corvette made the same jump that year from dream stage to reality.

Beyond the various styling tricks that came and went during the fifties, the decade also hosted

250 HP Chrysler New Yorker Deluxe St. Regis in Navajo Orange and Desert Sand

ANNOUNCING America's most smartly different car

CHRYSLER FOR 1955
WITH THE NEW 100-MILLION-DOLLAR LOOK

Everything about this dazzling Chrysler is completely new and dramatically different. It brings you a totally *new* fashion in modern motor car design.

The new Chrysler is inches lower in its sweeping silhouette . . . washed free of clutter . . . purposeful as an arrow shot from a bow. Its sleek new 100-Million-Dollar Look will make you feel like a hundred million dollars the instant you step inside!

And in performance this magnificent new Chrysler stands above all others. All

Chryslers *are* now V-8 *powered* with engines up to 250 HP . . . with Power-Flite, the only *fully-automatic* no-clutch drive that works without jerking or "time lag" . . . with the added safety of Power Brakes and the feather-light control of Chrysler *Full-time* coaxial Power Steering.

No other car on the road can offer you such an exciting sense of personal *power* and personal *pride.* Visit your Chrysler dealer today and see why now, more than ever before, *the power of leadership is yours in a Chrysler.*

to more than a few total image transformations. Most prominent perhaps was Chrysler's in 1955. Thanks to styling wizard Virgil Exner and his "Forward Look," all of the corporation's divisions benefited greatly from a complete makeover that year. From Chrysler's all-new "100 Million Dollar Look," right on down through DeSoto, Dodge, and Plymouth, the weakest of Detroit's Big Three took a big shot at reversing its fortunes by taking on a thoroughly modern image.

Gaining the most was Plymouth, a low-priced player that just one year before was boring buyers to death with its plain practicality. Under Exner's direction, Plymouth stylist Maury Baldwin created an award-winning restyle, which, when combined with the division's first overhead-valve V-8, helped bring many a customer back from the dead. Although commonly overlooked due to Chevrolet's similar rebirth that year, Plymouth's 1955 resurgence represented one of the greatest turnarounds of the decade in a year ripe with seemingly magical recoveries.

Nineteen-fifty-five may well represent the greatest turning point in modern American automotive history. Along with Chrysler's about-

Above
Even though Chrysler engineers had first equipped their cars with one of Detroit's top power sources, the fabled "hemi-head" V-8, in 1951, dull styling and a boring image slowed down sales considerably as the fifties progressed. But all of the corporation's divisions received astonishing face lifts in 1955, and Chrysler wasn't ashamed of bragging about just how much it spent on its all-new models—they didn't call it the "100 Million Dollar Look" for nothing.

Right
When introduced in 1954, Mercury's "glass-top" Sun Valley was based on the Monterey line and came in only two semi-off-the-wall colors, pale yellow or mint green. A new flagship, the Montclair, became the new base for Mercury's second-edition Sun Valley in 1955, when buyers could chose from any paint scheme offered. Only 1,787 Montclair Sun Valleys were built.

Left
All Chrysler's divisions featured new faces in 1955 as DeSoto, Dodge, and Plymouth rode the coattails of Virgil Exner's "100 Million Dollar Look." In the lesser lines, the new style was known as the "Forward Look," an image boldly demonstrated by this 1955 Dodge Royal hardtop, a marked departure from its 1954 forerunner. Complementing the fresh restyle in this case is a set of dealer-installed wire wheels.

Life magazine called it "the birth of a mechanical miracle . . . the most exciting idea in automobile design since Ford presented the first two-door sedan in 1915." "It" was Ford's 1957 Skyliner "Retractable" hardtop, a car that could be transformed from a full-fledged coupe into a convertible at the flick of a switch, a process that involved ten power relays, ten limit switches, eight circuit breakers, four lock motors, three drive motors and 610 feet of wire. Ford offered the intriguing Retractables up through 1959. This example wears a non-standard paint scheme based on Ford's original Retractable prototype.

face, Chevrolet made its legendary move into the modern market by, like Plymouth, combining an all-new OHV V-8 with stunning new styling, both features coming most unexpectedly in the low-priced field. At the other end of the scale, independent luxury marque Packard also rolled out a totally new body and its first OHV V-8, along with an innovative chassis featuring torsion bar suspen- sion. OHV V-8 power debuted as well under the hoods of 1955 Pontiacs, which would follow corporate cousin Chevrolet towards a more youthful market. As for Ford, 1955 was the year Dearborn introduced a concept known as personal luxury in the form of the classic two-seat Thunderbird.

The back half of the decade was marked by a new trend towards longer, lower, wider looks, an

Like Chevrolet's 1957 Bel Air, Ford's early Thunderbirds are easily recognized today by even the most casual observers. Truncated two-seat renditions of Ford's mainline 1955 and 1956 models, the T-bird grew slightly in 1957 thanks to a longer tail section wearing more pronounced fins.

image first—and probably best—embodied by Exner's 1957 Chrysler products. Other attempts to jump on the bandwagon weren't quite as successful, as Chevrolet, Buick, Oldsmobile, and Pontiac in 1958 grew much bigger but not exactly better, while Lincolns and Mercurys went right off the scale into the gargantuan category. But even before the ink on its 1958 restyle blueprints had had a chance to dry, GM was rethinking its stance, resulting in Bunkie Knudsen's Wide Track Pontiacs of 1959.

Knudsen, GM's youngest-ever general manager when he joined Pontiac in 1956, had been steadily pushing his once-stuffy division into a new, youthful light, both from an image perspective and through actual performance. Under his

Many a wag in 1958 wagered whether or not General Motors had made chrome an exterior color choice all its own that year as dazzling brightwork dominated all GM divisions' offerings. A little less garish than Oldsmobile's 1958 models, Buick's topline Limited was still no stranger to ostentatious display, especially up front where that "Fashion-Aire Dynastar" grille featured 160 individual chrome squares, "the better to blind you with."

This baby can flick its tail at anything on the road!

DE SOTO FIREFLITE 4-DOOR SEDAN IN SLATONE BLUE AND WHITE

Take the wheel of a new De Soto, and pilot her out through traffic toward the open road. Before you turn your second corner, you'll know you're driving the most exciting car in the world today. Here are some of the reasons why:

New *Torsion-Aire* ride! You get an amazingly level ride with De Soto's new suspension—Torsion-Aire. You take corners without sway...stop without "dive."

New *TorqueFlite* transmission! Most advanced ever built. Gives a smooth flow of power, exciting getaway!

New *Triple-Range* push-button control! Simply touch a button and *go!* Positive mechanical control.

New *Flight Sweep* styling! The new shape of motion—upswept tail fins, low lines, and 32% more glass area.

New super-powered V-8 engines! De Soto engine designs are efficient and powerful! (Up to 295 hp.)

Drive a new De Soto before you decide. You'll be glad you did. De Soto Division, Chrysler Corporation.

Wide new price range...starts close to the lowest!

FIRESWEEP—big-value newcomer—priced just above the lowest. 245 hp

FIREDOME—medium-priced pacemaker—exciting performance. 270 hp

FIREFLITE—high-powered luxury—the last word in design and power. 295 hp

DE SOTO

...the most exciting car in the world today!

De Soto dealers present *Groucho Marx* in "You Bet Your Life" on NBC radio and TV

From an armchair perspective more than three decades down the road, DeSoto's late-fifties offerings may appear a bit too much. But considering just how wild things had become on Detroit's styling front by 1957, the DeSoto look that year was relatively sleek and understated. Even with those sky-high fins, overall lines were light and flowing, and bodysides were clean and uncluttered. Compared to GM cars of 1957 and 1958, Chrysler Corporation's 1957 look was certainly easier on the eyes.

direction, Pontiac's design crew took Exner's long, low, and wide ideal and gave it an unmistakable identity. Wide Track wasn't just a name, it was the way in which the all-new 1959 Pontiacs dominated the road. Of course, GM's other divisions relied on similar platforms that year, and it wasn't long before Ford was copying the concept. But Pontiac was the progenitor. What Cadillac had done for car buyers' hopes leading into the fifties, Pontiac's Wide Tracks did similarly for customers awaiting what lay ahead in the sixties.

Between the two rolled a long parade of certified classics and milestones, cars that today stand on their own merits as automotive history makers for various reasons. In the styling category, there was Studebaker's almost timeless Starliner coupe of 1953, Chrysler's regal 1955–56 Imperial, and Lincoln's stunning Continental Mark IIs of 1956 and 1957. True ground-breakers appeared in the form of "America's only sports car," the Corvette, and the aforementioned two-seat Thunderbirds of 1955–57. And from a "market-wise" viewpoint, there will always be Chevrolet's 1955 Bel Air, the so-called "Hot One," the car that introduced performance to low-priced buyers.

Other lesser known vehicles deserve a kudo or two as well. Ford's Crestliner of 1950–51 was loaded with style thanks to its two-tone paint scheme and vinyl roof. Nash's original Rambler of 1950, to a degree, pioneered compact car production in this country and would have undoubtedly made a bigger splash in another time when small would not be a dirty word. Then there were curiosities like Mercury's 1954–55 Sun Valley,

with its green-shaded plexiglass roof section. A similar model was available from Ford through 1956. When it was dropped, its name, Skyliner, was attached to an even stranger concoction, this one featuring a fully retractable hardtop that tucked away beneath the rear deck, transforming a steel-roofed coupe into a convertible at the flick of a switch. Like the see-through roof, Ford's retractable top also faded away after three years.

Another supposedly better idea from Dearborn debuted in 1958, only to disappear within three years. A victim more of bad timing than of bungling, as is often suggested, the Edsel emerged right in the middle of a national recession. It also debuted at a time when trends were moving away from the garish, overdone treatments that had marked late-fifties styling up to that point. Today, it is certainly easy to laugh at that so-called "horse-collar" grille, but not everyone got the joke thirty-six years ago. Although it did fall far short of the 100,000 sales plateau Ford had hoped for, the 1958 Edsel did find 63,000 buyers, a respectable figure that surpassed even Chrysler division's total for the year. As an all-new model line, however, the 1958 Edsel's market performance left Ford flat, and it seems that every critic since has stood by ready to make sure Dearborn never forgets.

A cosmic payback? With so many wonderful automotive memories produced during the decade's earlier years, it seemed a bit unfair to end on such a downer. But then, that was the fifties; a little of this, a lot of that, and just enough of what makes history worth remembering.

Although Pontiac would end up with all the attention for its long and low Wide Tracks in 1959, it was stylist Virgil Exner at Chrysler Corporation who first brought the look to the forefront in 1957. As with all Chrysler's divisions, Dodge models for 1958 used the same bodyshell seen the year before with only minor trim adjustments, the most notable being a switch to quad headlights. This 1958 Dodge is a Coronet Lancer, the latter being the honorable name given all of Dodge's desirable pillarless hardtop models, four-door or two-door.

Another undeniable icon of the fifties was Cadillac's 1959 models with their enormous fins, bullet taillights, and extensive trim trickery. One of 11,130 built, this 1959 Series 62 convertible cost $5,455 thirty-five years ago, roughly a dollar and a dime per pound.

With so much attention given to Chevrolet's "Hot One," few seem to remember today that Plymouth's all-new 1955 offering was every bit as fresh and exciting. Like Chevy, Chrysler's lowest-priced models also received a modern OHV V-8 that year, along with an eye-catching restyle. Plymouth's new look was attractive enough to earn "The Most Beautiful Car of the Year" by the Society of Illustrators, the first time that society had extended an award to the automotive field in its fifty-three-year history.

Pontiac was just beginning to shake off its stuffy, stodgy image when Semon E. "Bunkie" Knudsen became its general manager in 1956. A modern OHV V-8 in 1955 had begun the turnaround; once Bunkie started moving and shaking, that transformation truly started taking shape, resulting in the trend-setting "Wide Tracks" of 1959. Expanding on the long, low, and wide ideal stylist Virgil Exner had first applied to Chrysler products in 1957, Pontiac's Wide Tracks instantly became all the rage—*Motor Trend's* editors were so impressed they bestowed the new line with their coveted "Car of the Year" award.

Ford Motor Company turned down the volume slightly on Edsel styling in 1959, but it still couldn't stop a slide for the division that had began life in 1958. After about 45,000 1959 Edsels were built, Ford feebly rolled out, however briefly, one last edition for 1960 before closing the door on a chapter Dearborn would've just as soon not written in the first place.

Chapter 2

Speed Merchants

Fifties Automakers
Were No Strangers to Performance

As much as America loves to remember the fifties—the music, the clothes, the cars—some details of those supposedly happier days, believe it or not, have been nearly forgotten. From an automotive history perspective, it has become all too easy these days to believe that performance—true ground-pounding, tire-melting, motorized muscle—wasn't invented until the sixties, basically because most horsepower hounds today never look back much beyond 1964, the year Pontiac introduced its ground-breaking GTO. What a concept—alotta engine in not alotta car. As far as most definitions of the modern "muscle car" read, PMD's go-getting "Goat" was the car that, thirty-something years ago, did start it all.

American automakers, however, had been running a horsepower race long before General Motors engineers discovered the obvious truth that drop-

ping their largest V-8s into their lightweight intermediate bodies represented the easiest, least expensive way to get from point A to B in a hurry. Granted, performance developments in the mid-sixties did overshadow essentially everything that came before, but that didn't mean car buyers in the fifties were strangers to speed. Quickness, responsiveness, road handling, and stopping power; now that was another story. Learning curves, however, do have to start somewhere, and as far as power-packed automotive engineering was concerned, the early fifties was as good as place as any.

In the beginning there was pure speed. Period. Performance in 1950 was measured simply and succinctly by how fast a car would go on the top end—how long it took to reach that maximum level mattered little. Of course, as any schoolboy at the time knew, the magical triple-digit barrier

Only 300 Corvettes were built in a limited production run for 1953. Chevrolet tried again in 1954 with a nearly identical model, this time offering it in black,

Pennant Red, and Sportsman Blue, along with the Polo White, the sole exterior choice the previous year.

"ROCKET"!
HYDRA-MATIC!

"88"

Oldsmobile has <u>both</u>!

The famous high-compression "Rocket" Engine—plus new Oldsmobile Hydra-Matic Drive*!

Try this thrilling combination at your nearest Oldsmobile dealer's!

Above, Oldsmobile "88" Holiday Coupé.
Hydra-Matic Drive optional at extra cost on all Oldsmobile models.

A GENERAL MOTORS VALUE

OLDSMOBILE

General Motors, without a doubt, held Detroit's hottest hand as the fifties began, both from a styling and engineering standpoint. Oldsmobile, benefiting from GM engineering's development of high-compression, overhead-valve V-8s, became the car to beat on the street in 1949. With a 303ci Rocket V-8 under the hood, the moderately sized Olds 88 was a muscular performer. And while rivals were toying with "semi-automatics" or still developing a workable automatic transmission design, Oldsmobile had GM's proven Hydra-Matic Drive, Detroit's pioneer in shiftless driving. Hydra-Matic first appeared as an option for the 1940 Olds.

Before Chevrolet's high-winding 265ci OHV V-8 made its way under fiberglass hoods in 1955, this 235ci six-cylinder was the only Corvette power source. Fed by three Carter carburetors, the Blue Flame Six made 150 maximum horses at 4200rpm.

was the mark of a truly hot machine, although few automobiles actually made that grade, and those that did took their sweet time getting there.

Early performance was also purely a function of price, as power and prestige went hand in hand. Physical laws being the same in most states, big, heavy cars needed big, powerful engines to get things rolling. In 1950, they didn't come much bigger and heavier than Cadillac, nor did they come any more powerful, thanks to GM's modern 331ci OHV V-8, introduced the year

before. Among other things, overhead valves made for better breathing characteristics and allowed engineers to improve volumetric efficiency through superior combustion chamber designs. While all other automakers were still relying on antiquated "flathead" engines with their valves situated within the cylinder block, it was GM's trend-setting, high-compression OHV V-8 that opened the door to all-new levels of power and efficiency.

At 160 hp, Cadillac's OHV V-8 may have been the fifties first power king, but it was corporate cousin Oldsmobile that probably deserves credit for building, if you will, the decade's first "muscle car." Predating Pontiac's GTO by fifteen years, Oldsmobile's Rocket 88 combined GM's cutting-edge underhood technology in a lighter, more nimble, less expensive package than Cadillac offered. The Rocket 88 debuted in 1949, featured all-new "Futuramic" styling and a 303ci OHV V-8 delivering 135 very healthy horses. Sporting a then-exceptional power-to-weight ratio of roughly one horsepower for every 22.5 pounds, the Olds Rocket 88 was revered as the strongest thing running on Main Street, U.S.A in 1950. Olds Rockets also quickly became a dominant force on the fledgling

Chevrolet's Corvette wasn't this country's only fiberglass two-seater in 1954. Independent Kaiser also took a shot at the sports car market that year with its Darrin roadster, a curious machine that suffered from poor body quality, a weak powerplant (Willys' 90hp six-cylinder), and the plain fact that Kaiser at the time was all but dead in the American market. Only 435 were built.

In keeping with Kaiser's penchant for off-the-wall design, the Darrin sportster featured sliding doors that simply disappeared into the front fenders.

National Association for Stock Car Auto Racing (NASCAR) circuit, founded by Bill France on the sands of Daytona Beach, Florida, in 1947.

Various other automakers soon followed GM's lead, adopting OHV V-8 technology as the only way to keep up in what was rapidly developing into a hell-bent-for-leather horsepower race. Studebaker introduced an OHV V-8 in 1951, followed by Lincoln in 1952, and Ford and Mercury in 1954.

Among these, Lincoln's advancement was easily the most dramatic, as a fresh, resized bodyshell was combined with a revamped chassis featuring new ball-joint front suspension, resulting in a luxury cruiser that could turn heads in more ways than one, thanks in part to its 160hp 317ci V-8. Like the Olds Rocket, the 1952 Lincoln was as much at home on the track as the boulevard, a fact demonstrated in impressive fashion during Mexico's "Carrera Pan Americana,"

The 1954 Kaiser Darrin possessed two major drawbacks. Its fiberglass body tended to show ripples and crack quite easily, and its standard 90hp Willys flathead six-cylinder engine wasn't exactly up to the task of competing with

Detroit's other two-seat fiberglass sports car. But daring souls who wanted more power were in luck as some of the last cars were retrofitted with big, brawny Cadillac V-8s.

the grueling 1,900-mile endurance run first held in 1950. From 1952 to 1954, specially prepared Lincolns dominated their class in the often-fatal—for both drivers and spectators alike—"Mexican Road Race," which was open to stock, factory-equipped automobiles from all over the world. A host of engineering improvements, including Lincoln's first four-barrel carburetor, helped up output in 1953 to 205 hp, five less than Cadillac.

But as far as challengers to Cadillac's early

prominence atop Detroit's powerful pecking order were concerned, Chrysler had beaten 'em all out of the gates in 1951, introducing a totally different kind of overhead-valve engine. Chrysler engineers called it their "Firepower V-8," an appropriate name for a powerplant that would 15 years later evolve into the hottest muscle machine the sixties offered. Equal in both displacement (331ci) and compression (7.5:1) to Cadillac's big OHV post-war pioneer, the Firepower V-8 featured an intrigu-

Beginning in 1951, Hudson's stepdown Hornet was the king of the fledgling NASCAR stock car racing circuit, thanks both to it overall ruggedness, as well as its unbeatable, unbreakable six-cylinder powerplant. This reproduction of one of those "Fabulous Hudson Hornets" is part of the NASCAR history display in Daytona Beach's Klassix Auto Museum.

ing cylinder head design that, like overhead valves themselves, wasn't anything new on the automotive scene, but was certainly something to brag about in its latest form.

Combustion chambers were hemispherically shaped—as opposed to the typical wedge-type layout—with a centrally located spark plug and canted valves actuated by rocker arms mounted on parallel rocker shafts. Everything about the way the so-called "hemi head" worked—breathing,

flame propagation, volumetric efficiency—was superior. Weight was the only drawback as the heads were quite large. High output, however, easily offset the added pounds—at 180 hp, Chrysler's Firepower V-8 became Detroit's new horsepower leader in 1951.

DeSoto introduced its 160hp "Firedome" hemi in 1952 and Dodge followed with a 140hp version one year later. Once between the fenders of the lighter Dodge models, Chrysler's formidable

Even though it was an antiquated "flathead" competing against a host of modern OHV V-8s, Hudson's impressive 308ci six-cylinder was more than capable of throwing its weight around with a vengeance. Introduced in 1953, the Twin-H power option used dual carbs to help squeeze 160 horses out of the Hudson six. This is a 1954 Twin-H power Hudson, which was upgraded to 170hp.

hemi started setting speed records almost everywhere it went, amassing 196 AAA stock car standards during Utah's Salt Flats trials at Bonneville in September 1953.

As the old gearhead adage goes, "racing improves the breed," and so it was that nearly all automakers in the fifties were busy running all-out on tracks and in time trials in attempts to prove to potential buyers just how much their cars had improved. Along with such prominent Big Three players as Dodge, Lincoln, and Oldsmobile, independent Hudson was a checkered flag regular. Beginning in 1951, Hudson passed Olds to become NASCAR's driving force as the "Fabulous Hudson Hornets" raced to victory after victory, all without the benefit of thoroughly modern overhead valves. Or a V-8.

Up through 1954, Hudson's rugged, "stepdown" Hornets ruled NASCAR not by relying on all-new technology, but by making maximum use

Smart way to go places...

THE *Studebaker Speedster*

Relying on the neo-classic bodyshell introduced in 1953, Studebaker entered the sports touring field in 1955 with its President Speedster. Sure, the optional tri-tone paint and the huge chrome bumper may have been a bit much, but the Speedster did represent an attractive package for the lively set with its engine-turned dash, full instrumentation, and simulated wire wheel covers.

of long-standing, durable equipment. The Hornet's sting came from a 308ci side-valve six-cylinder pumping out loads of steady torque, along with 145 horses. That figure jumped to 160 in 1953 when the fabled "Twin H-Power" dual-carb option was added. By 1954, the updated 170hp Twin H-

It wasn't the biggest, it wasn't the strongest, but Chevy's 265ci OHV V-8, introduced in 1955, was the first really hot powerplant in the low-priced field. With a simple, lightweight ball-stud rocker arm design borrowed from Pontiac, the 265 V-8 could rev with the best of 'em. Maximum power of 162 horsepower (with a four-barrel carburetor) came on at 4400rpm. Compression, at 8:1, was relatively high for its day.

Power Hornet was surpassed only by Lincoln and Cadillac as far as horsepower-per-cubic-inches was concerned—and the Hudson managed this feat with two less cylinders than its rivals.

Hudson wasn't the only company in the fifties to compete without a V-8. GM's lowest priced player, Chevrolet, also had no choice but to stick with its time-honored straight six when styling mogul Harley Earl and engineering chief Ed Cole decided to introduce this country's first true sports car.

Chevrolet's Corvette was one of four GM Motorama showcars that literally rolled off a rotating stage in 1953 right into regular production. Powered by a triple-carbureted 235ci "Blue Flame" six, the little two-seat Corvette rushed from rest to 60mph in roughly 11sec, a laudable feat at the time.

Cole's engineering team trimmed more than two seconds from that figure in 1955 by installing Chevrolet's new 265ci OHV V-8, pumped up to 195hp, into the Corvette equation. And things really started heating up once Zora Arkus-Duntov got his hands on the car. A revised chassis, riding beneath a restyled fiberglass shell, appeared in 1956 along with a twin-carb 265 V-8 rated at 225 hp. Adding the optional, race-only "Duntov cam" pushed maximum output to an unofficial 240 horses. Big news, however, came the following year when fuel injection debuted atop the Corvette's enlarged 283ci small-block V-8. In maximum tune, the so-called "fuelie" 283 produced 283hp—one horsepower per cubic inch. Calling the 283hp 283 "an absolute jewel," *Road & Track* reported a startling 5.7sec 0-60mph pass for the 1957 fuelie Corvette—quick performance even by today's standards.

Attempts to rival Chevrolet's Corvette never quite made the cut. Most memorable was another fiberglass-bodied two-seater, the Kaiser Darrin,

While Chevrolet was turning heads in 1955 with its totally new overhead-valve V-8, Dodge was impressing buyers a few steps up the price ladder with its powerful "hemi-head" V-8, a division trademark since 1953. At the top of the heap, Dodge's optional Super Red Ram V-8 featured a Carter four-barrel carburetor, dual exhausts, and 7.6:1 compression. Output was 193hp. Chrysler Corporation's hemi V-8s easily dominated Detroit's horsepower race in the fifties.

By 1957, Chevrolet was offering a wide range of power levels in its V-8 passenger cars, beginning at 185 hp, produced by Chevy's two-barrel 283ci small-block. The top carbureted option was the 270hp 283 with its twin four-barrels. But for the buyer who truly wanted it all, there was the fuel-injected 283 transplanted from the Corvette. Two versions were offered, a 250hp version with 9.5:1 compression and a 283hp screamer with 10.5:1 pistons.

built briefly in 1954. Even if hadn't been hindered by its underpowered, 90hp Willys six-cylinder powerplant, this stylish, Dutch Darrin-designed sportster would've undoubtedly been doomed by its lame duck status—by the time the Kaiser Darrin made it to market, the parent company was all but finished on the American scene. Only 435 Darrins—each featuring those unforgettable slid-

ing doors—were built before Kaiser-Willys left the U.S. in 1955 for South America.

Fellow independent Studebaker also briefly offered a sporty model, although it wasn't exactly a direct competitor for the Corvette. Studebaker had hoped to build a two-seat convertible, but after that plan failed, the reasonably sexy President Speedster hardtop was rolled out in 1955.

Chevrolet's Rochester-supplied Ramjet fuel injection system was originally the work of engineer John Dolza, who first produced a working unit in 1955. Once chief engineer Ed Cole put Zora Arkus-Duntov on the project in 1956, things really started cooking. Fuel injection was offered as the top Corvette power option from 1957 to 1965. Passenger cars were built with the optional Ramjet 283s as well in 1957, with a few also so equipped in 1958 and 1959.

Simulated wire wheel covers, foglamps and tri-tone paint dressed up the outside, while full instrumentation—including an 8000rpm tachometer—in an engine-turned dash were part of the deal inside. Power came from a 185hp 259ci V-8, with either a three-speed manual or automatic transmission available. Zero to 60mph times were recorded in less than 10sec and top end was about 110 mph. Not bad at all, but the Speedster still couldn't avert oblivion. Like the Kaiser Darrin, it too was a one-year wonder, leaving the Corvette to continue as "America's only sports car," a once-shaky claim that basically became a stone-cold reality by the end of the decade.

But another claim made by Chevrolet hype masters concerning their fantastic plastic two-seater wasn't true at all, although many reporters today still erroneously repeat it as fact. As much as Chevy fans would like to think that the 1957 Corvette's fuel-injected small-block was Detroit's first power-plant to reach the supposedly magical one-horse-power-per-cubic-inch level, it wasn't. That honor actually belongs to Chrysler's "beautiful brute," the 300 letter-series models. One year before Chevrolet introduced its Rochester fuel injection equipment, Chrysler customers could've equipped their 300B

Above
Ford Motor Company fans who thought the 1952-1954 Lincolns were hot luxury bombs had another coming once Chrysler introduced its letter-series models in 1955. With a 300hp hemi-head V-8 beneath the

hood, the lavish 1955 C-300 emerged as Detroit's most powerful production car, and could easily run with anything on the road. An exciting restyle in 1957 fit the equally exciting 300C to a tee.

Right
Following the C-300's 300hp 331ci hemi was an even more powerful 354ci version for the 300B in 1956. Top optional power for the 300B was 355 hp, making Chrysler's luxury cruiser Detroit's first car to offer more than

one horsepower per cubic inch. In 1957, the 392ci hemi (shown here) pumped out 375 horses in standard form. For $500 more, additional compression (10:1) and a high-lift cam upped the 300C's output ante to 390 hp.

Chevrolet's push into the performance field beginning in 1955 left Ford little choice but to follow. In 1957, Dearborn began offering a racing-inspired dual-carb 312ci Y-block for both its standard line and Thunderbird models. That, however, was by no means the end of it. This 1957 Fairlane is equipped with the rare supercharged 312, an option that, along with Ford's twin four-barrels, was quickly deleted once the Automobile Manufacturers Association stepped in to cut factory ties to racing early in 1957.

Identified by its E-code, Ford's dual-carb 312 produced 270hp in 1957, while this F-code Y-block pumped out 300hp with the help of a McCulloch centrifugal supercharger supplied by Paxton. A special NASCAR racing kit reportedly upped the F-code 312's output to 340hp.

hardtops with an optional 354ci hemi V-8 rated at 355 horsepower—even by today's math it isn't too tough to determine that that measures out to a tad more than one pony per cube.

Chrysler's 300 letter cars, appropriately enough, drew their name from the original model's horsepower rating—in 1955, the C-300 became Detroit's first 300hp automobile. Supplying all that power was the already proven 331ci hemi, this one featuring twin four-barrel carburetors, 8.5:1 compression and a serious solid-lifter cam. A beast beneath the hood, the C-300 was a beauty every-

where else with an attractive Imperial "egg-crate" grille up front and a standard leather interior inside. Raw performance didn't come any classier in the fifties. Nor in the sixties or seventies for that matter.

Following the 1955 C-300 came the 300B in 1956, 300C in 1957, and so on. As mentioned, the 331 hemi grew to 354ci for the 300B (standard 354 hemi output was 340hp), then jumped to 392 cubes in 1957, and finally to a whopping 413ci beneath the 1959 300E's long, long hood. Top optional output for the 300 in the fifties was 390 horses in both 1957 and 1958. No other

After the one-year wonder President Speedster came and went in 1955, Studebaker entered the sporting market again in 1956, introducing the Golden Hawk, a reasonably attractive package powered by Packard's muscular 275hp 352ci V-8. But all that cast-iron power up front also meant much unwanted weight, a plain fact that didn't help promote the Golden Hawk as a sports car. Enter the 1957 Golden Hawk with a 289ci Studebaker V-8 in place of the big Packard powerplant. To make up for the decrease in cubic inches, engineers planted a McCulloch supercharger atop the "Sweepstakes" V-8 as standard equipment for the Golden Hawk, which, like the Speedster before it, also featured a sporty engine-turned dash and full Stewart-Warner instrumentation. Supercharged Golden Hawks were built for both 1957 and 1958.

fifties-era Detroit automaker even came close to that power level.

Then again, all that muscle didn't come cheap—the gut-wrenching 300 letter cars were not only not for the faint of heart, they weren't for the faint of wallet, either. But if you preferred hemi performance without all that high-priced luxury, there was Dodge's D500 models, introduced in 1956. Aimed at sanctioned competition, Dodge's first D500 option included a potent 260hp 315ci hemi in a polite package that didn't exactly turn heads at the club like its 300 cousins, but could certainly twist a few off trackside on the NASCAR circuit. Various levels of D500 and Super D500 performance were offered each year up through the end of the decade.

The same year Dodge debuted the D500, DeSoto and Plymouth also introduced a pair of hot offerings, each heavily loaded with exclusive imagery along with ample performance. DeSoto's 1956 Adventurer was adorned with a contrasting eggshell white and gold finish, while power was supplied by a 320hp 341 hemi. Even at roughly 3,800lb, the Adventurer was a solid screamer, reportedly going from 0 to 60mph in about 10sec. Although its exclusivity diminished slightly the fol-

At 275 hp, Studebaker's blown 289 V-8 was as powerful as the Packard V-8 it replaced, yet weighed in at 100lb less, meaning the 1957 Golden Hawk handled much better than its 1956 forerunner. Maximum boost supplied by the belt-driven Jet Stream supercharger was 5psi. To compensate for that added intake pressure, compression in the Golden Hawk's V-8 was dropped from the standard 289's 8.3:1 to 7.8:1.

lowing year, the high-powered Adventurer continued as DeSoto's flagship into the sixties.

Plymouth's Fury was also a limited-edition, high-profile performer initially only offered in one shade, again eggshell white with gold accents. But in Plymouth's case, a hemi was not available; in its place was what was known as a "poly-head" V-8, an engine named for its polyspherical-shaped combustion chambers. Exclusive to the 1956 Fury was a 240hp 303ci poly-head power-plant. Much lighter than its gold-and-white DeSoto counterpart, Plymouth's Fury could hit 60mph from rest in 9sec. And unlike the Adventurer, the Fury remained an exclusive, one-finish-only offering up through 1958. In 1959, the once-coveted Fury nameplate was downgraded to yeoman duty among an entire model line, while the Sport Fury became Plymouth's top image machine.

The Impala Convertible—long, low and loaded

NOTHING GOES WITH SPRINGTIME LIKE A BRIGHT NEW CHEVY! *Here are cars to rejoice in ... sports-minded, fun-hearted and beautiful as all outdoors. The way they perform, ride and handle makes for the happiest driving you've ever known. Got spring fever? Trade it for that Chevrolet feeling!*

There's something about these new Chevies that was made to order for the warm, wonderful days ahead.

You can see it in the eagerness of their low-thrusting silhouettes. You can feel it in the spirited way they take to an open stretch of highway, in the nimble way they negotiate a winding country road.

These are ears to rejoice in—the surest, happiest cure ever invented for an old-fashioned case of spring fever. And the treatment becomes habit-forming with your first close-up look at the gull-wing glamor of that all-new Body by Fisher.

Every one of these new Chevrolet passenger cars is lower, wider and more luxurious in every detail. And every one is loaded with engineering advances that make driving more restful and zestful. Give some rein to the radically new Turbo-Thrust V8,* for instance, and see how it loves to shrink the miles out where they're long and lonesome. Or follow your wanderlust down a dipping backwoodsroad—and feel the putting-green smoothness of Chevrolet's new kind of ride.

Your local dealer will be glad to fill you in on all the details—including prices as low as Chevy's roofline! ... Chevrolet Division of General Motors, Detroit 2, Michigan.

*Optional at extra cost.

The dashing Corvette—America's only authentic sports car.

CHEVROLET

The Bel Air Sport Coupe—every window of every Chevrolet is Safety Plate Glass.

By 1958, Chevrolet's passenger car line had grown considerably, while the fabled Corvette was easily the hottest thing rolling out of Detroit. To get those big Impalas moving, engineers turned to the new "W-head" 348ci Turbo-Thrust V-8, the forerunner to the famed 409. Maximum Corvette power in 1958 came from a fuel-injected 283ci small-block rated at 290 horsepower in top tune.

Discounting exclusive imagery, throwing aside all that extra-curricular equipment that only added to a car's bottom line, the hottest performance news of the fifties was without a doubt "The Hot One." Chevy's all-new 1955 Bel Air with its equally new optional OHV V-8 may not have been the most powerful, or even the fastest car of its day, but it was the most affordable performance machine available. Before Chevrolet's high-winding 265ci V-8 hit the scene, buyers in the low-priced field could only watch as wealthier customers hogged all the high-powered fun. And the first modern V-8 Chevy was only the beginning.

In 1956, Chevrolet passed some of the Corvette's power onto the passenger car ranks as the dual-carb 265 became an option, helping inspire *Mechanix Illustrated's* Tom McCahill to call the 1956 Chevy the "best performance buy in the world." "Chevrolet has come up with a poor man's answer to a hot Ferrari," continued McCahill. "Here's an engine that can wind up tighter than the E string on an East Laplander's mandolin—well beyond 6000 rpm—without

Introduced in 1956, Dodge's potent D500 engine option was offered with an eye towards NASCAR competition, but the package nonetheless appeared on everything from mundane four-doors to sexy convertibles. This exceptionally rare 1957 Coronet D500 convertible is one of about 3,000 D500s built from 1956 to 1961. With a 285hp 325ci D500 V-8, a 1957 Dodge could do 0–60mph in 8.5sec, according to *Sports Car Illustrated*.

blowing up like a pigeon egg in shotgun barrel." Optional fuel injection made the 1957 Chevy even hotter as maximum power reached 283 hp.

Chevrolet's corporate cousin Pontiac also turned to fuel injection in 1957 for their limited-edition Bonneville convertible. Featuring a 310hp 347ci fuel injected powerplant, the Bonneville droptop was intended as a high-profile announcement to the American market that Pontiac was no longer an old man's car company. Along with the big, brawny Bonneville, Pontiac also offered an intriguing induction option in 1957 known as "Tri Power," a triple-carburetor setup that was similar to Oldsmobile's legendary J2 equipment.

Exotic induction pieces were relatively common in the fifties. Along with Chevrolet and Chrysler, Packard, Cadillac, and Ford offered dual four-barrels, the latter fitted to both Dearborn's passenger cars and its two-seat Thunderbird for a brief time in 1957 before the Automobile Manufacturers Association's so-called "ban" on factory racing support. The AMA edict also shot down Ford's optional supercharged 312 Y-block, an engine that would've landed the high-flying T-bird right alongside Chevrolet's Corvette. Centrifugal supercharging was also tried by, of all automakers, Kaiser (in 1954 and 1955), as well as Studebaker in its Golden Hawk of 1957 and '58.

Plymouth built its limited-edition Fury from 1956 to 1958, each year preserving the exclusive image by offering the car with only one exterior appearance package. Eggshell White was the sole paint scheme in 1956; in 1957 and 1958 it was Buckskin Beige.

Either way, all three Fury hardtops were adorned with loads of gold trim, inside and out. Beneath the hood of this 1958 Fury is a gold-painted "Dual Fury V-800" V-8, a high-performance 318ci dual-carb engine that produced 295hp.

Triple carburetion appeared again among GM ranks in 1958 when Chevrolet introduced its 348ci "W-head" V-8, a bigger, more powerful engine to motivate a bigger, bulkier Chevy. The 348, forerunner of Chevrolet's fabled 409, had begun life as a truck powerplant, then developed into an honest-to-goodness performance option for a model line that was no longer based on a lithe, relatively compact bodyshell as it had been prior to 1958.

But by the late fifties, the bigger-is-better ideal had come to dominate Detroit's thinking. While nearly all cars grew in both size and weight so too did engine displacements and power outputs. As the decade came to a close, 400ci was not out of the ordinary and the 400hp barrier was just waiting to be broken. Clearly, much performance groundwork had been laid, leaving it up to a new generation of sixties movers and shakers to grab the baton and pick up the pace. That they did.

While DeSoto's first Adventurer in 1956 featured an exclusive gold-trimmed look like Plymouth's Fury, color choices were expanded for models to follow. The last high-powered, limited-edition Adventurer was built in 1959, the year DeSoto introduced optional swivel bucket seats. This 1959 Adventurer coupe, one of 590 built (ninety-seven convertibles were also produced), is powered by a 350hp 383ci V-8 fed by twin Carter four-barrel carburetors.

With its distinctive valve covers resembling a "W," Chevrolet's so-called "W-head" 348 Turbo-Thrust V-8 debuted in 1958 to help keep Chevy's bigger, heavier models in step with the times. Mounting one four-barrel carburetor in standard form, the first 348 produced 250 horsepower. Adding the three Rochester two-barrels shown here pushed output up to 280 hp.

Chapter 3

Declaration of Independents

One Step Beyond the Big Three

Decisions, decisions. These days, the seemingly endless list of automotive marques, both foreign and domestic, awaiting new car buyers in this country can, and often does, boggle the mind. Whether you're looking for an affordable compact, all-purpose utility vehicle, high-powered sportster, or loaded luxo-mobile, the choices are as plentiful as they've ever been during most of our lifetimes. It wasn't all that long ago we had it relatively easy come new model time. As late as the seventies, other than those pesky imports and maybe a lightly regarded American Motors machine or two, it was basically the Big Three or nothing at all.

Of course there are still some among us who can remember a distant time when you needed the proverbial scorecard to tell the various American automotive players apart. Although cut down considerably by the Great War that was supposed to end all wars, the U.S. automaker line-up of the twenties still made today's far-flung four-wheeled empire look like small potatoes in comparison. So many cars, so little time. Names like Auburn, Apperson, Chalmers, Cord, Duesenberg, Graham-Paige, Marmon, Moon, Peerless, Pierce-Arrow, Stutz, Westcott, Winton—and these were but a few of the more popular makes. Many, many other lesser nameplates were also present and accounted for, however briefly.

Then along came a melting pot of sorts called

Although Kaiser hype-masters preferred to promote their 1953 Dragon as a hardtop, it was obviously a four-door sedan. Helping evoke the hardtop "mirage" was a standard vinyl roof that created a continuous delineation above the side windows. The typical post was still there, but who would notice, right? A trim option introduced in 1951, the Dragon image became a model all its own for 1953. Introduced on Halloween 1952, the Dragon featured a heavy dose of what Kaiser liked to call "Bambu" vinyl. Along with the roof, Bambu vinyl also covered various interior panels, the package shelf, seat trim, and dash, and even was found in the trunk and glove box. Wire wheels were optional, while 13-karat gold-plated trim was standard 1953 Dragon fare.

the Great Depression, a national economic disaster that claimed many once-great carmakers along with countless other businesses. By the time another global war arose to wake up the American economy, Detroit's automaking giants, General Motors, Ford, and Chrysler, were solidly entrenched as the "Big Three," while all other surviving rivals were simply "independents." Like the Big Three, those independents strong enough to ride out the Depression years were all treated to a piece of the defense contract pie during World War II. And as peace neared, President Franklin D. Roosevelt made it clear that the wealth would remain spread around after the war, proclaiming that any and all independent automakers would be given every chance within his wide powers to compete with the big boys.

Prominent proof of what F.D.R. had in mind before his death in April 1945 quickly appeared in the form of the Kaiser-Frazer Corporation, a newborn independent incorporated in August that year. Founded by former Graham-Paige Motors Corporation president Joe Frazer and powerful ship builder Henry Kaiser, Kaiser-Frazer joined this country's automaking fraternity in a big way, setting up shop in the huge Willow Run facility outside Detroit, courtesy of a Reconstruction Finance Corporation lease. One of the world's largest buildings at the time, the Willow Run plant had been constructed by Ford Motor

White sidewall tires and wheel discs available on all models at extra cost

Presenting the "next look" in cars

NEW 1950 STUDEBAKER

Success breeds success! The car that led in modern design now moves still more spectacularly out ahead!

The new 1950 Studebaker is here—and you can see at a glance that it's America's "next look" in cars.

Here's the dramatic and unexpected sequel to the tremendously popular "new look" in cars that Studebaker originated three years ago.

Here's a truly inspired 1950 Studebaker—dynamically new in form and substance—America's most advanced new car—styled ahead and engineered ahead for years to come.

Paced by a breath-taking new Studebaker Champion in the low-price field, this is a complete line of completely new 1950 Studebakers.

Each one is increased in wheelbase length and over all length—thrill-packed with the new performance of higher compression power —comfort-cushioned with self-stabilizing new Studebaker coil springs.

Discriminating America is giving the 1950 Studebaker an enthusiastic welcome. Stop in at a nearby Studebaker showroom the first chance you have. See the 1950 Studebaker —the "next look" in cars!

©1949, The Studebaker Corporation, South Bend 27, Indiana, U. S. A.

Studebaker was more than happy to tell the world in 1947 that it was the "first by far with a postwar car." Three years later, after nearly all other automakers had left South Bend in the dust, Studebaker began barking again after rolling out another new car. But while the company's first modern postwar models had brought buyers running by the proverbial droves, the next step up the ladder into 1950 left many witnesses scratching their heads. "Which way is it going?" was one of the more popular comments.

Henry J styling was interesting to say the least, especially for a low-priced budget machine. This 1953 Corsair rolls on non-stock, owner-installed modern tires. Total Henry J production in 1953 was 16,672; only 1,123 the following year.

Company in 1940 to manufacture bombers for the war effort. Moving into Willow Run certainly represented a coup of sorts for Henry Kaiser and Joe Frazer, but it was just one of many rapid, major steps towards what appeared as a very promising future, at least from a late-forties perspective. Time, however, would soon tell the true tale.

After beating the Big Three out of the postwar blocks with an all-new, modern model, this one featuring stunning slabside styling, K-F jumped to the top of the independent heap in 1947, outselling even established Studebaker, Nash, Hudson, and Packard. But as the fifties dawned, Kaiser-Frazer was already on a downhill slide, due to a malady already well known among the independent crowd—the bucks simply weren't big

General Motors wasn't the only automaker in 1953 to roll a dream car image right off the stage onto the street. Packard's sexy 1953 Caribbean convertible was a direct descendant of designer Richard Arbib's 1952 Packard Pan American show car. Unable to channel the body like Arbib did, Packard stylist Dick Teague nonetheless added a nice array of personal touches to the Caribbean to help set it apart from the standard line. Included was a hood with a functional scoop, fully rounded rear wheelwells and a continental spare tire in back. Dazzling wire wheels also helped add to the distinctive look. Only 750 Caribbean convertibles were built in 1953, followed by 400 in 1954. An all-new body and tri-tone paint arrived for the Caribbean in 1955, when 500 models were sold. Production of the final rendition in 1956 was 276 convertibles, 263 coupes.

enough to allow continued competition with the much wealthier automaking powers. After selling 144,507 cars in 1947, K-F sales peaked at 181,316 the following year, rallied briefly at 146,911 in 1950, then dropped steadily; 99,343 in 1951, 75,292 in 1952, and 21,686 in 1953. Frazer, the higher-priced of the two parallel model lines, disappeared entirely after 1951, leaving Kaiser to struggle on alone, albeit briefly.

As early as 1951, Henry Kaiser had begun talks with Willys-Overland chief Ward Canaday concerning the purchase of Canaday's firm, which had been in and out of operation through various partner- and directorships in Toledo, Ohio, dating back to 1907. Probably best known for its hard-working "Jeeps," Willys kicked off the postwar era by also offering utilitarian station wagons, then introduced the practical, playful Jeepster in 1948.

YOU'VE NEVER SEEN ANYTHING LIKE IT!

Touch a button—it's a super-safe open car! Push a button—there's the comfort of a family sedan! It's the Nash Rambler Landau... America's lowest-price 5-passenger Convertible!

Come see the most thrilling convertible in years—the new Nash Rambler!

For the first time—all the fun and sun of a super-smart open car, *with the safety of Airflyte Construction*—combined with the year-round comfort and rattle-proof rigidity of a sedan. All at a quick button's push—all at *lowest-price!*

Goes like a blue streak! Easiest of all to handle! Delivers *up to 30 miles a gallon* at average highway speed.

Custom-tailored to your order . . . equipped with Weather Eye, radio—nearly $300 worth of custom extras *at no added cost!* Come see the new Nash Rambler that's got America talking Nash!

IT'S THE NEWEST MEMBER OF THE *Nash* FAMILY
Airflyte

THE AMBASSADOR • THE STATESMAN • THE RAMBLER CONVERTIBLE LANDAU
Great Cars Since 1902
Nash Motors, Division Nash-Kelvinator Corporation, Detroit, Michigan

Statesman
More than **25 miles** to the gallon at average highway speed! Like the Nash Ambassador, the Statesman Super and Custom series feature coil-springing on all four wheels . . . Sky-Lounge Safety Interiors, Airliner Reclining Seat . . . Twin Beds . . . and America's best aerodynamic design, proved by wind-tunnel test to cut fuel cost, wind-noise, fatigue.

Ambassador
The most modern of America's fine cars now offers Hydra-Matic Drive with exclusive Nash Selecto-Lift Starting. America's top high-compression performance (7.3 to 1 ratio) on regular gasoline.

All Nash cars have Airflyte Construction . . . Body and frame one-welded, super-strong unit that's rattle-proof, twice as rigid, stays new years longer.

THERE'S MUCH OF TOMORROW   IN ALL NASH DOES TODAY

Willys re-entered the passenger-car market in 1952, rolling out its innovative "Aero" line, very attractive, easy-to-handle little cars that were at the same time reasonably roomy and politely compact.

In the summer of 1953, Kaiser bought Willys, with all Kaiser-Willys production eventually relocating to Toledo as the coveted Willow Run facility was sold to GM. It was, however, the beginning of the end, at least as far as American customers were concerned. Not even a pooling of resources could prevent the inevitable, and Kaiser-Willys pulled up stakes in 1955 then moved to Argentina.

Although it was a short stay in the U.S. market for Kaiser it certainly wasn't uneventful. Intriguing offerings included a four-door hardtop, a four-door convertible, and what may well be considered this country's first hatchback, the Traveller. Innovative models also included the compact Henry J, introduced in 1951, and the sleek 1954 Darrin two-seater, America's other fiberglass sports car. And as far as looks were con-

---

Nash may well have copped honors for the most alarming all-new postwar design when it introduced its Airflyte line in 1949. Like the later Edsel, these "bathtub" Nash models have since found a place in countless comedic skits, but innovative aspects of the aerodynamic Airflyte was nothing to laugh at; it was easily the most efficient shape produced in the early

fifties, if not the entire decade. And if cutting-edge aerodynamics weren't your cup of tea, there was also Nash's little Rambler, a car that debuted in 1950 as Detroit's first relatively successful compact. Nash even went so far as to offer a convertible Rambler, which could drop its top but had to leave the window frames and rails in place.

Before Nash had debuted its compact Rambler in 1950, Powel Crosley, Jr. was this country's main small-thinking automaker, and to this day his cars easily rank right down there with the smallest ever built in America. In back to the left is a 1951 Crosley sedan. Crosley also built station wagons and open sports cars before discontinuing production early in 1952. The yellow curiosity in front is a 1950 Skorpion, a custom-bodied Crosley featuring a fiberglass roadster shell originally marketed by the Wilro Corporation of Pasadena, California. On the right stands one of Crosley's competitors, the "mail-order" King Midget, a kit car produced in Athens, Ohio, from 1947 to 1970. This red 1958 King Midget is one of 5,000 sold during the company's twenty-three year run.

Small cars were one thing, but small utility vehicles? Introduced in August 1950, Crosley's diminutive Farm-O-Road was "designed to do big jobs on small farms—or smaller jobs on big farms." Optional Farm-O-Road equipment included a pickup bed with or without a hydraulic dump mechanism, front and rear power take-offs, and a hydraulic drawbar in back for mounting various implements. Among the latter were a 10-inch plow, rake, spike and disc harrows, planter, seeder, cultivator, and two mowers, a standard unit and a large, three-gang commercial affair. Later in 1959, Crofton Marine Engineering, in San Diego, California, brought Crosley's Farm-O-Road back to life, producing identical models called the Crofton Bug and Brawny Bug.

cerned, Kaiser-Frazer didn't take a back seat to anyone.

Even with a limited budget relative to the Big Three, K-F did manage to stay close to Detroit styling's cutting edge, thanks to, among others, veteran designer Howard "Dutch" Darrin, of pre-war Packard fame. If onlookers thought the first Kaisers and Frazers were attractive, they had another thing coming once a Darrin-inspired restyle appeared in 1951. Problem was, that body, like the one that had debuted late in 1946, had to last far too long for its own good. Once buyers became bored with the look, the Kaiser was just another car left in the dust by the Big

The 1951 Frazer 4-door Sedan shows the clean, new beauty of the spear-motif design. Its wondrously low price makes the Frazer the fine-car buy of '51!

The 1951 Frazer Vagabond—the famous 2-cars-in-1—converts in 10 seconds from luxurious 6-passenger sedan to spacious carrier...for sports or business equipment!

five new handcrafted body styles 1 9 5 1

FRAZER

Truly built to better the best on the road, the 1951 Frazers are handcrafted—with regally rich interiors in a wide variety of exclusive colors and fabrics. All models are powered with the new Supersonic High-Torque Engine. Hydra-Matic Drive, optional at extra cost.

The Pride of Willow Run

The 1951 Frazer Convertible America's only 4-door convertible has added convenience, comfort, spaciousness and visibility...of course a fully automatic top!

The 1951 Frazer Manhattan comes in *two* models—one with its metal top coated in glamorous colors, the other with its top covered in shimmering nylon. Either way enhances to the utmost the convertible look in solid steel.

©1950 KAISER-FRAZER SALES CORP.

Three. Among other things, Kaiser never did overcome the lack of a modern OHV V-8, a stumbling block that didn't trip up Studebaker.

Self-proclaimed as the "first by far with a postwar car," Studebaker had followed up its all-new 1947 model with an even more alarming restyle in 1950, a look that left many critics without a straight face. Wags continually asked which way the "bullet-nose" 1950 Studebaker was going, a reaction to the coupe's wraparound rear glass that seemingly echoed the pointed nature of the car's front end. Kibitzers, however, stopped laughing in 1951 when Studebaker debuted a modern OHV V-8, quite an achievement for the independent automaker that had begun life building farm wagons in South Bend, Indiana, nearly 100 years before.

Like Kaiser, Studebaker relied on high-profile styling in an attempt to lure buyers away from the Big Three fold. Although Raymond Loewy often receives sole credit for Studebaker's trendy appearance, it was young stylists under Loewy's direction like Virgil Exner (before he went on to bigger and better things at Chrysler) and Robert Bourke who actually did the bulk of the pencil work. That work included the neoclassic 1953 Starliner hardtop, as clean and sleek

Like Nash, Kaiser-Frazer was no stranger to innovative design. After plans to offer a front-wheel-drive car fell through, Joe Frazer and Henry Kaiser set their sights a bit lower and still managed to amaze many onlookers with their models' creativeness. Intriguing offerings, shown here in this 1951 Frazer ad, included a four-door hardtop, Detroit's only four-door convertible at the time (which, like the Rambler, went topless with its window

rails still in place), and the industry's first hatchback. Kaiser also offered a hatchback, the Traveler, and a similar four-door hardtop, the Virginian. But all this creativeness aside, nothing could change the realities of competition, and cash-strapped Frazer didn't survive much longer than it took for the ink on this advertisement to dry.

In 1947, Studebaker had emerged as one of this country's first automakers with a truly new postwar car. But by 1950, the newness had worn off, leaving the South Bend, Indiana, independent no choice but to go back to the drawing board. Stylist Robert Bourke of

Raymond Loewy's design studio supplied a facelift for 1950. Front or rear, the 1950 Studebaker easily represented a love it or hate it proposition.
Earl Davis photo

a look as any automaker, established or independent, unveiled in the fifties.

But as much as Bourke's beautiful bodyshell—sometimes called the "Loewy coupe"—was worthy of praise in 1953, it, like the Kaiser restyle of 1951, ended up being over-used as it reappeared in slightly dressed-up form each succeeding year. Being an independent, Studebaker was not immune to the aforementioned cash-crunch malady. Retooling expenses simply proved too great. Whereas GM, Ford, and Chrysler could afford to spend tens of millions of dollars on a new model every three or four years, their various rivals couldn't. And also like

Kaiser, Studebaker officials soon found themselves looking for strength in numbers.

In June 1954, Studebaker's Harold Vance and Paul Hoffman met with Packard's James Nance to announce the latter independent automaker's purchase of the 102-year-old South Bend firm. Once-proud Packard, a Detroit pioneer and builder of high-line automobiles that had been, just twenty-some years before, rivaling the classic Duesenbergs as the finest machines this country could offer, found itself outclassed in the fifties as Cadillac, then Lincoln sped away with all-new looks and updated engineering.

As if the 1950 Studebaker's pointed "spinner" nose didn't attract enough attention—both positive and negative—the wraparound rear glass helped inspire many a wag to ask, "which way is it going?"
Earl Davis photo

Packard was the first independent to offer a modern automatic transmission—Ultramatic—in 1949, but its 1950 "bathtub" body remained tied to pre-war tastes, and its antiquated straight-eight L-head was out-and-out old news. Restyled sheet metal in 1951, followed again by another modern remake in 1955—this one riding atop an all-new torsion-bar chassis mounting an equally new, powerful OHV V-8—couldn't make up for lost time. Or respect. After selling 104,5937 luxury models in 1949, Packard sales fluctuated mildly, then dropped like a rock to 27,307 in 1954.

Nance needed someone to help him pay the intimidating bill for the 1955 model's total transformation, thus the deal with Studebaker, itself a company in dire need of some extra cash. As it turned out, the Studebaker purchase only succeeded in dragging Packard down to its death; in July 1956, the Curtiss-Wright Corporation took over troubled Studebaker-Packard, Nance resigned soon after, and Packard operations in Detroit ceased in August. Even though the Studebaker-Packard corporate name carried on into the sixties, the last Packards—glorified Studebakers wearing different trim and badges, as they had since 1957—rolled off the South Bend line in July 1958.

Hudson saved the best for last as far as its excellent stepdown chassis models were concerned. Introduced in 1948, the stepdown Hudsons lasted up through 1954 before Hudson was transformed into "Hash" after the company's merger with Nash. Perhaps one of the mid-fifties most attractive models, the 1954 Hornet easily made for Detroit's sleekest four-door sedan with its long, low lines, a direct product of the stepdown design.

A bad deal on Nance's part? Actually he had originally hoped to save the day for Packard by tying the Studebaker-Packard agreement into an even bigger merger, this one to fall in line under George Mason's American Motors banner. Mason, head man at Nash-Kelvinator in Kenosha, Wisconsin, was the main mind behind the scheme, which involved uniting the major independents to maximize their strengths, all in an effort to better compete with the Big Three. The first part of his plan became official on April 22, 1954, when Nash and fellow veteran independent Hudson merged.

Under Mason's visionary direction, Nash had

One of the most coveted engineering features of the fifties was the modern overhead-valve V-8, a design that left the age-old "side-valve" flatheads in the dust. OHV V-8s truly came into their own in 1955, the year low-price rivals Chevrolet and Plymouth introduced theirs, joined by Pontiac and independent Packard. Displacing 352ci, Packard's new OHV V-8 came far too late to turn the once-proud marque's fortunes around.

become a pioneer in compact car production, introducing the little Rambler in March 1950 and the even smaller Metropolitan four years later. And although many then, and since, have laughed at Nash's total postwar restyle in 1949, the "Airflyte" line's superb aerodynamics, as well as its innovative unit-body construction, was no joke. On the other side of the coin, Hudson built typically large automobiles, but had also left the mainstream in 1948 with its rugged "stepdown" design, itself uti-lizing unitized body-frame construction. Mason's American Motors merger, however, brought an end to the stepdown Hudson as AMC production was consolidated at Nash's Kenosha works, where much of the 1955 Nash look, as well as its engineering, was transformed into a totally new Hudson, a model sometimes unflatteringly labeled a "Hash." The last stepdown left Hudson's old Jefferson Avenue factory in Detroit on October 29, 1954.

As for the second half of the American Motors

With one last lunge before his company was dragged down to death by Studebaker, James Nance vainly attempted to bring Packard into the thoroughly modern fifties in 1955, spending everything his company had (and much of what it didn't) on an attractive restyle, a new overhead-valve V-8, and an innovative chassis that featured long torsion bars in place of conventional springs for all four wheels.

plot, Mason did apparently intend to join his Hudson-Nash co-op with Studebaker-Packard once James Nance had finalized that deal, but the idea never got beyond the talking stage. Although reasons for the failure are varied, the prime stumbling block came October 8, 1954, when George Mason died of pneumonia. Mason's replacement atop American Motors, George Romney, wanted no part of yet another merger with two obviously ailing automakers. And that was that. Studebaker-Packard limped on towards eventual death in the

sixties, while Romney's American Motors was born again in 1958 as the decision was made to unceremoniously dump the Nash and Hudson lines and stick only with the compact Rambler, a move that proved right in step with the times. By 1960, even the Big Three were building small cars.

In the sixties, light, agile, practical compacts would finally come into their own after literally decades of disinterest had left various automakers holding the bag following attempts to market small cars. During the fifties, few buyers even considered

Portrait of Craftsmanship in Action

The all new *Packard Hawk*

THE MOST ORIGINAL CAR ON THE AMERICAN ROAD

You will find no other car like the Packard Hawk. It is the most original and distinctive automobile crafted in America, styled to match the tempo of our times. Its unique flowing lines are aerodynamic. Its fins: functional. It is designed with that imaginative flair you only expect to find in Europe's most fashionable automobiles. Faithful to its thoroughbred breeding, the Packard Hawk is a *luxury* automobile with smooth, soft leather seats and elegant, tasteful interior appointments.

Extra Power from Built-in Supercharger

Its appearance is complemented by power from a highly efficient V-8 engine with a built-in supercharger, capable of instantaneous acceleration, or smooth performance under the most trying conditions of stop-and-go traffic. The supercharger with variable speed drive cuts in automatically as needed, for acceleration or extra power for passing or hill climbing, but when not in use, costs nothing extra in gasoline. It is a design for power, with economy.

The Packard Hawk is *the* new car with a regal air that immediately distinguishes its owner as a man of position. Put yourself in that position . . . behind the wheel of a Packard Hawk, soon.

Studebaker-Packard offers the most varied line of cars in America. See them all . . . economy cars . . . sports cars . . . station wagons . . . luxury sedans and hardtops.

Visit your Studebaker-Packard dealer today!

Studebaker-Packard
CORPORATION
Where pride of Workmanship comes first!

Above
Basically a Nash with Hudson nameplates added, the 1955 Hornet represented the beginning of the end for a once-proud independent that had ably battled its much larger Detroit rivals throughout the early fifties. One of

4,449 V-8 Hornet four-door sedans built for 1955, this model is also equipped with air conditioning, a rare, as well as high-priced option in those days.

Left
While Nash and Hudson were moving in together to form AMC, Studebaker and Packard were setting up shop under one roof in South Bend, Indiana. Sadly for the once-great luxury marque, the same thing that happened to Hudson also happened to Packard. After 1956, Packards were nothing more than rebadged

Studebakers. And in the case of the odd 1957 Packard Hawk, the badge wasn't the only thing changed. Basically a Studebaker Hawk with an awful extended nose tacked on, Packard's Hawk soared only with turkeys. Luckily, South Bend officials saw fit to put the Packard nameplate to rest in 1958.

Designed by stylist Phil Wright and engineer Clyde Paton, Willys attractive Aero line debuted in 1952. Attractive both in form and function, the easy-to-handle Aero models might have met a better fate in another time and as a product of another automaker. As it was, Willys merged with troubled Kaiser in 1953, then headed south to Argentina with its parent company in 1955. This is an Aero Lark, one of six different Aero lines offered by Kaiser-Willys in 1954.

small cars, basically because most believed what they were told—bigger was better, right? Nonetheless, more than one attempt was made to convince customers that affordable compacts were the wave of the future. As mentioned, of these efforts, Nash probably showed the greatest success, although Henry Kaiser certainly gave it one helluva try with his pint-sized Henry J of 1951–54.

But if you want to talk small cars, really small cars, they didn't come much smaller than Crosley. Refrigerator mogul, radio magnate, owner of the National League Cincinnati Reds baseball team,

Powel Crosley first offered his somewhat odd, certainly tiny "car for the forgotten man" in 1939. When Crosley's compact creations reappeared in 1946, they weighed only 1,150lb, rolled on an 80in wheelbase, and cost less than $1,000. Innovations in 1949 included four-wheel disc brakes and the so-called "COBRA" four-cylinder engine, the name coming from its copper-brazed sheet metal cylinder block. Neither the brakes nor the Cobra engine were without their bugs, but that didn't stop Crosley from continued creativeness.

That same year Crosley introduced the Hot

Shortly before his death in 1954, George Mason merged Nash and Hudson into American Motors, a move that effectively ended Hudson's identity as the cars themselves merged with Nash in both form and function. By 1957, that form was truly something to catch the eye—for whatever reason is your call.

Shot, a sports car that not only didn't have a top, but lacked doors, as well. In 1950, the Super Hot Shot, or Super Sport, appeared with doors. To Powel Crosley's delight, a Super Sport appeared at Sebring, Florida, in 1950 for the inaugural 12-hour endurance classic and finished first as far as the "Index of Performance" was concerned. Along with the Super Sport, Crosley also rolled out the Farm-O-Road utility vehicle in 1950, which was able to both plow the fields and haul the family to the hoe-down, perhaps in style depending on your outlook. But neither glorified riding lawn mowers or race-winning roller skates could keep Powel Crosley in the carmaking business— his Marion, Indiana, plant shut down in July 1952. Luckily he knew how to sell refrigerators and radios.

Various other independents, diminutive or otherwise, came and went during the fifties; most are barely worth mentioning. As for the prominent ones, the decade represented a make-or-break proposition, a situation that couldn't have made Detroit's dug-in Big Three any happier.

Always one to step out from the crowd, Henry J. Kaiser transformed his interest in a "people's car" ideal into a sheet metal reality in 1951, then named the car after himself. The little Henry J turned many heads early on; 82,000 were sold the first year. But like the Kaiser company itself, Henry J's Henry J quickly faded from the scene then disappeared completely after 1954.

It's Here! Nash Presents a Completely New Kind of Car ...the Metropolitan!

Four years ago we presented for public opinion the prototype of an entirely new kind of car . . . an <u>American</u> concept of European motor car design. It was seen by hundreds of thousands of enthusiastic motorists across the nation. Their opinions have gone into the car we present today . . . the all-new Metropolitan. It is revolutionary in economy and operating costs, new in handling ease, and thoroughly American in comfort and performance. Read about it here . . . then accept our cordial invitation to see and drive the Metropolitan.

No MATTER WHAT car you are driving now, you'll want to see and drive the exciting new Metropolitan. The result of 11 years' research by Nash—an entirely new kind of car, a *new size of* car for today's driving needs!

It's a family car . . . practical for small families, a sensible second car for large families . . . offering up to 40 miles to the gallon!

It's a pleasure car . . . a dashing, road-hugging *sportster* . . . exciting to drive . . . proudly styled, beautifully made . . . and handles like a sports car.

It's a business car, perfect for those who use a car constantly—and want *lowest* operating costs and amazing parking ease.

Come and see the finest and most luxurious car of its size ever built. A car that can ride three in front, with an extra utility seat in back.

Here's more good news! Whether you choose the Convertible or the "Hardtop" model, the low, *low* price *includes* Weather Eye Conditioned Air System, custom radio, directional signals, continental rear tire mount, foam rubber cushions with custom nylon and genuine leather upholstery. There's nothing more to buy!

Yes, the Metropolitan is *all automobile.* Built as a double-rigid structure—protecting you with unitized Nash Airflyte Construction. Built with Nash quality—Nash ruggedness—and completely bonderized for rust protection. Built like all Nash cars for a double lifetime of service.

We invite you to see and try this exciting new kind of automobile—sold and serviced by Nash dealers everywhere. Then you'll know why everybody's talking about the new Metropolitan.

SOLD AND SERVICED BY NASH DEALERS FROM COAST TO COAST

HOLIDAY/APRIL

UP TO 40 MILES A GALLON!

- Official records in 24-hour NASCAR supervised runs: Non-stop economy test —41.6 miles a gallon at 34.7 m.p.h. Performance test—1469 miles at an *average* of 61 m.p.h.
- Choice of two models—Convertible and "Hardtop"
- Powered by the famous Austin A-40 overhead valve engine
- Continental Styling on a new scale
- World's Easiest Handling and Parking
- Riding Comfort of a Large Car
- Airflyte Unitized Construction— World's strongest and safest
- Lowest of Operating Costs

Metropolitan

NEWEST MEMBER OF THE

Nash

Airflyte Family

Ambassador · Statesman · Rambler

Built with a "Double Lifetime" . . . Your Safest Investment Today . . . Your Soundest Resale Value Tomorrow

---

Nash-Kelvinator's George Mason tended to think small in big ways. First came the 1950 Rambler. Then in 1954, Nash introduced the truly small Metropolitan, a car perfect, in Mason's mind, for the congested byways of the rapidly growing American suburbs. In 1959, Metropolitan sales had reached an amazing 22,000 units. Nonetheless, the car was dead by 1962.

Chapter 4

Carrying The Load

Not All Memorable Machines of the Fifties Were Cars

Almost lost among the seemingly endless roll call of unforgettable passenger cars built in the fifties is a lengthy list of notable utility vehicles; station wagons and trucks that, at the very least, helped American buyers change the way they looked at station wagons and trucks. Once relegated to the mundane workaday world, both forms of transportation experienced a transformation akin to Cinderella's on the night of the big dance as style, status, and prestige were injected into what had historically been a purely practical equation.

Station wagons had not exactly been strangers to the good life before the fifties began, as a few had been aimed at the tea and crumpet set, who often needed a hard-working second

Chevrolet's most expensive model, at $2,857, the Nomad wagon returned for its last appearance in 1957, when 6,534 were built. Pontiac also ended its two-door Safari run that year after building 1,292 1957 models. Both divisions, however, continued using the once-exclusive nameplates on conventional four-door wagons.

vehicle to, perhaps, haul the wife's tennis partners and their gear to the club. But even though some station wagons had shown up in the luxury car ranks, nearly all wagons in the early-fifties were spartan, to say the least. Most featured wood-framed bodies, a quaint if not primitive throwback to an earlier, less technologically developed time.

Indicative of just how primitive things could be in the thoroughly modern postwar era were the "woodie" wagons offered by Willys—simple, low-priced, bare-bones transportation built with cargo hauling first and foremost in mind. But while Willys was attempting to keep prices—as well as expenses—down by rolling out an essentially identical woodie wagon year after year, Detroit's big boys were tooling up for a change as the fifties dawned, trading troublesome wood for low-maintenance all-steel bodies. And not only did the new steel wagon bodies insure better quality (less rattles, more durable), they also lent themselves easily to the same styling touches applied to the passenger car lines.

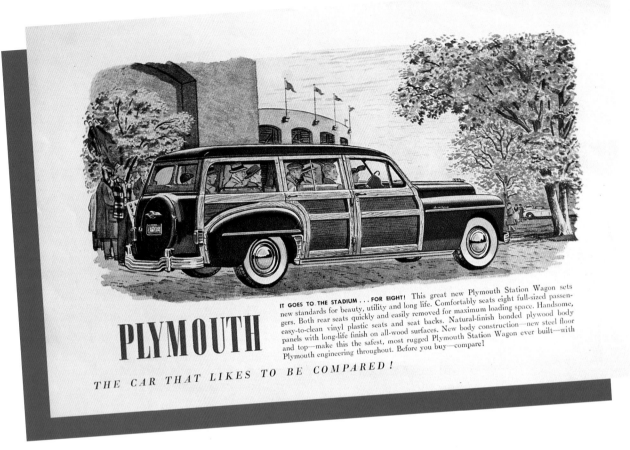

IT GOES TO THE STADIUM . . . FOR EIGHT! This great new Plymouth Station Wagon sets new standards for beauty, utility and long life. Comfortably seats eight full-sized passengers. Both rear seats quickly and easily removed for maximum loading space. Handsome, easy-to-clean vinyl plastic seats and seat backs. Natural-finish bonded plywood body panels with long-life finish on all-wood surfaces. New body construction—new steel floor and top—make this the safest, most rugged Plymouth Station Wagon ever built—with Plymouth engineering throughout. Before you buy—compare!

PLYMOUTH

THE CAR THAT LIKES TO BE COMPARED!

Before the fifties, station wagons were all "woodies," in that they used wood-framed bodies, a cheap, easy way for any and all automakers to market cargo-carrying renditions of their passenger line cars. But during the decade's early years, Detroit began dropping the wood bodies in favor of all-steel wagon construction, which didn't rot, swell, or become termite infested. Rust, however, was another story.

General Motors seemed especially endeared to classy wagon production, and by 1957 was manufacturing various four-door pillarless hardtop versions that could both catch the eye and bring home the groceries. The pillarless hardtop, an all-new postwar styling trend introduced in regular production by GM in 1949 (Chrysler had tried the trick earlier in limited numbers), did away with the typical sedan's B-pillar—the "post" that cut the side glass area into front and rear sections—resulting in an open, airy look reminiscent of a ragtop. It was no coincidence that early hardtops were labeled "convertible coupes."

Whatever the name, a two-door hardtop still looked sweet, and it didn't take long for designers to add that look to four-door models, then station

Ford's first all-steel station wagon appeared for 1952, and reappeared in nearly identical fashion up through 1954. This Sheridan Blue 1954 Customline Ranch Wagon is powered by Ford's 130hp 239ci "Y-block," Dearborn's first modern overhead-valve V-8. Notice how the license plate was designed to swivel out as the tailgate went down.

wagons. Although American Motors was the first to build a pillarless hardtop wagon—the 1956 Rambler Custom Cross Country—there was no denying that Buick's stylish Caballero and Oldsmobile's Fiesta of 1957 were about as snazzy as it got among the four-door station wagon crowd. Less dazzling but equally trendy were the various four-door hardtop wagons introduced by Mercury that year.

But easily the most stylish among the fifties wagon crowd was Chevrolet's Nomad, a sporty two-door traveler introduced in 1955. Although two-door wagons were nothing new, the Nomad was certainly a ground-breaking creation, com-

bining youthful pizzazz and upscale prestige with all the purposeful utility typically offered by the yeoman family wagon. Critics with large families may have bemoaned the lack of an extra set of doors, but who really cared when the thing looked so darn good on the way to the corner store?

The work of Chevrolet styling studio head Claire MacKichan and stylist Carl Renner, the Nomad began life as one of three Corvette prototypes built for GM's 1954 Motorama show circuit. Key to the image was an attractive ribbed roof supported by light, forward-raked pillars, a design Renner penned. GM styling chief Harley Earl liked Renner's work so much, he had MacKichan apply the idea to Chevy's standard two-door station wagon for 1955. A regular-production version appeared in February.

Along with Renner's roofline with its wraparound side glass, the 1955 Nomad also featured exclusive bodyside spears, full rear wheel openings (passenger cars were "scalloped"), and seven vertical trim bars on the tailgate that, like the roof pillars, incorporated a distinctive forward rake. Next to nothing from the cowl back was shared with the standard wagon line. Inside, exclusive interior treatments included chrome headliner bows and special pleated upholstery with "waffled" inserts. Linoleum lined the rear cargo floor. Available with either the "Stovebolt" six-cylinder or Chevrolet's all-new 265ci OHV V-8, the Nomad wagon didn't come cheap—at roughly $2,500, a V-8-powered 1955 Nomad cost more than a Bel Air convertible.

High-priced or not, the classy Nomad returned in 1956, this time without the exclusive bodyside trim, special upholstery, and modified rear wheel openings. Even then, there was no mistaking the look, which returned one more time for 1957 before being dropped from the ranks at year's end. Chevrolet label makers opted to continue using the Nomad name—beginning in 1958 it was stuck on the more conventional four-door wagons—but it just wasn't the same.

Less renowned, yet of equal note was Pontiac's version of the Nomad, the Safari. Despite com-

How soon they forget. Or did they? In 1953, Oldsmobile image-makers had used the Fiesta name for an exclusive, limited-edition luxury showboat, a convertible cruiser that wouldn't have been caught dead hauling the Little League team to the park. Four years later, those Olds men dusted off the nameplate for their classy four-door hardtop wagon, undoubtedly as a way to tie in the new utility model with an existing high-profile image.

While Chevrolet's first Nomad shared a front clip with the standard passenger car line, much of the design from the cowl back was exclusive to the two-door sport wagon image. Special features included radiused rear wheel openings, a ribbed roof with forward-sloping pillars, and a canted tailgate with its ribbed trim.

plaints from Chevrolet people who wanted to keep the idea to themselves, Pontiac's movers and shakers were able to wrestle Renner's roofline away from MacKichan's studio and apply it to the two-door Chieftain 860 line, which rolled on a 122in wheelbase, seven inches longer than the Nomad. That difference, however, was all part of the plan as the Safari was intended to be a bigger, better Nomad.

Pontiac's 1955 Safari came standard with the division's first OHV V-8 (287ci) backed by a Hydra-Matic automatic transmission—no six-cylinders or three-speed manuals here, although a six could be requested. Few were. Standard Safari features also included leather upholstery and carpeting in the rear cargo area. Of course, all this added up to hefty asking price, some $500 more than the V-8 Nomad's bottom line. That aspect alone was enough to limit the Safari's appeal, nonetheless Pontiac followed Chevrolet's lead and offered the high-profile model up through 1957, when declining sales finally forced the issue. Like Chevrolet, Pontiac also continued using its once-exclusive nameplate on lesser machines after the sporty two-door Safari was dropped.

Always seemingly at the cutting edge, whether it was engineering, styling, or general design,

Unlike the 1956 and 1957 Nomads, Chevrolet's 1955 model was also equipped with exclusive interior treatments including "waffled" vinyl seat inserts. This particular fully loaded 1955 Nomad wagon features optional air conditioning, a luxury that cost upwards of $500 in the mid-fifties.

General Motors was also at the lead when it came time to transform the image of the American light-duty pickup truck. Much more so than station wagons, light trucks had really never been anything but light trucks before 1955. A cargo bed, a cab, sturdy ruggedness—what else did you need to haul manure down to the lower forty? Style, comfort, and class were basically never considered by truck buyers, at least not until Chevrolet rolled out its Cameo Carrier pickup.

B.C., "Before Cameo," pickups were purposefully plain, not pretty. Although some options were offered and color choices were available, most trucks on or off the road were devoid of creature comforts and were seemingly either black or dark green. Bumpers and most grilles were painted to match the body, and trim was basically non-existent, as was convenience. Then along came Chevrolet's Cameo to stir things up.

Introduced March 25, 1955, the elegant Cameo Carrier half-ton pickup was unlike anything truck buyers had ever seen. Detroit's first high-class hauler, the Cameo combined various car-like styling cues with all the utility typically found in a truck, although a buyer probably would've thought twice about dumping a load of manure into that stylish cargo bed with its cab-wide fiberglass sides. Abundant trim, attractive custom taillights, an airy cab featuring trendy wraparound glass, and an exclusive Bombay Ivory/Cardinal Red paint scheme made the classy Cameo Carrier tough to miss, whether parked at the club or sitting at a loading dock.

And just like that, trucks were no longer meant only for the Oshkosh B'gosh crowd. A touch of style outside, a little more comfort inside, maybe an optional automatic transmission—all these attractions and more quickly became pickup selling points after Chevrolet had shown customers a truck didn't have to be all work and no play. While the Cameo carried on for four years, Chevrolet's standard truck line was becoming an attraction in itself as more options, a higher level of trim, and even two-tone paint choices were made available, all advancements not overlooked by the competition.

While Ford never went so far as to offer anything as lavish as the Cameo, it did respond in 1957 with a slightly dressier pickup known as a "Styleside." Like the Cameo, Ford's Styleside trucks featured a trendy, clean-looking, cab-wide bed in place of the age-old pontoon rear fenders found on most trucks of the day. Chevrolet retaliated with its Fleetside models in 1958, the same year the Cameo was finally discontinued.

Not to be outdone, the Dodge boys replied with a stylish pickup of their own in 1957, and they didn't just rely on carline styling cues, they went right for the real thing. Introduced in May 1957, Dodge's so-called "Sweptside" pickup was, up front, a D100 half-ton truck, itself a restyled machine featuring hooded headlights, a new grille, and a trendy wraparound windshield (which had debuted in Dodge ranks two years before). In back, however, all bets were off as the Sweptside's cargo bed made even the Cameo's creative box pale in comparison.

While lower-priced Chevrolet and Pontiac shared the Nomad image, higher line Buick and Olds both offered stylish four-door hardtop station wagons in 1957. Buick's was the Caballero, a high-class hauler that featured "Riviera styling"—a reference to Buick's first use of the pillarless hardtop roofline—the 1950 Roadmaster Riviera coupe.

Then and now. The 1956 Ford F100 shown here is indicative of how bland pickups were during the decade's early years. Thirty-five years later, light-duty trucks were anything but dull, as this 1991 F150 XLT 4x4 demonstrates. Chevrolet first began adding true style and class to its pickups in 1955. Ford didn't respond until 1957.

Proving that you didn't always need a lot of money to turn a few heads in the car (or truck) business, Joe Berr, manager of Dodge truck's Special Equipment Group, simply had SEG employee Burt Nagos weld a pair of high-flying fins, taken off a 1957 Dodge Suburban two-door wagon, right on to the Sweptside's bed in place of those old, boring pontoons. Somewhat amazingly, the station wagon quarter panels, complete with those "signal tower taillights," fit like gloves, as

Chevrolet changed the pickup market forever in 1955 by introducing the Cameo Carrier, a stylish half-ton truck with a fiberglass bed and various car-like styling cues—notice the taillights and deluxe wheel covers. Offered only in an exclusive Bombay Ivory/Cardinal Red paint scheme, Chevy's first Cameo found 5,220 buyers. One of 1,452 Cameo's built in 1956, this polite pickup is powered by a six-cylinder—the dual exhaust system is an owner-installed feature. Additional Cameo paint choices were also added in 1956.

did the Suburban's rear bumper. Once a little extra trim was added to the cab to match the wagon's existing beltline brightwork and a somewhat crude cut-down tailgate was mounted between those sweeping fins, the job was done. Whether you liked the look or not, you couldn't knock Berr for at least trying to keep up with the Joneses.

Like its Cameo counterpart, Dodge's Sweptside was hindered by a high price and a limited market niche—stop and think, would you bang a

Yes, those are standard 1957 Dodge car quarter panels on this truck. Dodge designers created the 1957 "Sweptside" half-ton by simply welding Suburban station wagon rear sheet metal—complete with those unmistakable taillights—right onto the D100 pickup's cargo bed. A somewhat simple, cutdown tailgate, the Suburban's chrome rear bumpers, and matching trim for the cab completed the package.

toolbox over those fins? A certified novelty in 1957, the intriguing Sweptside reappeared in 1958 only to find few takers, then was quietly discontinued in January 1959. By then, Dodge's less eccentric, and certainly stylish "Sweptline" pickups had debuted to do battle with Ford's Stylesides and Chevrolet's Fleetsides. By 1960, a truck buyer was faced with a nice choice of half-ton trucks that looked good while working hard.

And if that buyer was truly adventurous, he could try out Ford's Ranchero, a curious vehicle that was half car, half truck. Both a ground-breaking attention-getter and a throwback to the prewar days when most light trucks were simply passenger car front ends followed by cargo beds, the Ranchero debuted in 1957 as "America's first work or play truck." But unlike its prewar ancestors, which were more truck than car underneath, Ford's 1957 Ranchero was very much a car, with the added convenience of a truck-type bed thrown in for good measure. Extra-cost Ranchero equipment included nearly all the comforts of home—

Although Chevrolet did offer its classy Cameo Carrier for four years, demand diminished considerably once the standard half-ton line was treated to a long line of comfort, convenience, and appearance options. This heavily loaded 1957 3100 pickup is equipped with a 283ci V-8 backed by a Hydra-Matic automatic transmission. Additional attractive features include two-tone paint (the white cab accent), various trim baubles, and deluxe wheel covers.

Ford kicked off the "car-truck" craze in 1957 with its first Ranchero, a vehicle that featured a convenient cargo bed but was far less truck than it was car. Both six-cylinder and V-8 power was available, as were an impressive list of convenience options such as power steering and brakes.

electric seats and windows, automatic transmission, power steering and brakes—while optional two-tone paint only made the package that much more attractive. Ford's 223ci "Mileage Maker" six-cylinder was standard, but a Y-block V-8 could be added for a few dollars more.

Not only did the Ranchero kick off a playful, practical legacy that continued into the sixties, it also inspired a rival counterpart from Chevrolet. Two years after Ford's "car-truck" debuted, Chevy introduced its El Camino, which was Spanish for "the road." Buyers who opted for Chevrolet's Ranchero response in 1959 found themselves hitting the hard road in style, at least as far as *Motor*

With Ford's gauntlet laid down, Chevrolet couldn't help but retaliate with a "car-truck" of its own. Introduced in 1959, Chevy's El Camino was built just one more year before being temporarily discontinued. Chevrolet would reintroduce the idea, on the all-new A-body Chevelle platform, in 1964.

Life's editors were concerned. In their words, "even the [El Camino's] cab has rakish lines— more so, one might say, than the Ranchero inasmuch as the rear window is not squared off but has a graceful forward slope." Although somewhat oversimplified, both car-trucks were essentially station wagons with the rear roofs removed. But in the El Camino's case, the chop job was done with a bit more grace compared to Ford's effort. Like the Ranchero, Chevrolet's El Camino continued on into the sixties with great success.

Ten years after it had begun, the fifties closed after bringing about change after change after change. And perhaps nowhere in the four-wheeled world were those changes more radical than among the practical transportation class, where rugged dependability and rawboned utility were reformed and fashioned into an attractive package basically taken for granted today. Comfort, convenience, cargo capacity, and class? Who woulda thunk it?

American car buyers of the fifties, that's who.

FIFTIES *Fins*

DENNIS DAVID

ACKNOWLEDGMENTS

Books like this are not written without the help of many others. Indeed it is through their assistance that I have been able to provide the reader with this in-depth look at Detroit's marvelous fins. I wish to thank my good friends and colleagues Kit Foster and Mike Lamm for their help and encouragement. They are two of the great automotive journalists of all time. My good friends Dr. Paul Sable, Mark Patrick, Jonathan Stein, and Don Keefe also contributed greatly to the endeavor. Thanks also to Bruce and Genia Wennerstrom, co-chairs of the Greenwich Concours de Elegance. Special thanks also to my editor, Keith Mathiowetz. The idea for *Fins* was his, but the pleasure was mine.

Special thanks to all of the car owners who willingly gave their time at all hours of the day in order to get that one special shot: Ralph Bortugno; Charles and Jo-Ann Kraynack; Bob Heuer; Rocco Mancini; John R. Cote; Douglas Marr; Jack and Barbara Lane; Wade Jacobs; Joe and Patrick Conetta; Karen Hubbell; Philip Ciaffaglione; Art Brucato Jr.; Noel and Starr Evans; Bob and Linda LaMadeleine; Jack and Pat David; Don and Ruth Jack; James and Arlene Hamelin; John and Pat Kelley; James Ricci; Paul and Linda Accarpio; Phil Lefebvre; Ralph Perillo; Don and Diane Bouchard; Albert Dellabianca; Donna Hohider; Charles Andrews; Bob and Priscilla Pepler; Ray Mitchell; Mike Davis; Tom Lorgrippo; Eric Stoldt; Neil Carrano; Todd Depino; Leo Boudreau; Bob Majeski; Tony Vespoli; Bud and Stasia Motuzick; Rick Cyr; Bernie Roselli; and Richard Hall.

Special thanks also to my good friend Nicholas E. Pagani, who owns several of the cars featured in this book. When not leasing a portion of his collection out to Hollywood movie projects, he found the time to make his cars available to me.

While this book is filled with the glamorous convertibles and hardtops that seem to define a beautiful car, it also features many sedans and station wagons. Too many books are written only to define a certain segment of the market, but I thought it was important to show that the fin was an intricate part of the automobile in any form.

I'd also like to offer special thanks to my proofreader, who also happens to be my beloved wife, Susan. It is said that everyone in this world has a soul mate. If this is true, then I have certainly found mine. Together we share many hopes and dreams of which this book is just one. I should also thank my special "Hershey Buddy," Chris, my son. Together we have walked countless miles at car shows all over the country. He shares my enthusiasm for the automobile and together we make a team. I wish to dedicate this book to my father, who has always been there for me with words of wisdom and encouragement.

INTRODUCTION

I t's hard to pinpoint exactly when it started. Some say it was the slip of a pen that resulted in a slight rise in the rear quarter panel of a Buick or a Cadillac. After all, the stale look of the immediate postwar American automobile was literally crying out for something new. After several years spent building war machines instead of automobiles, Detroit could do nothing more than dust off the old dies and start punching out cars in order to fill the nation's thirst for new automobiles. When that thirst was quenched, the motoring public began demanding more from Detroit. No longer would a car sell on the merits of its dependability alone. It had to have something new, it had to look different, and most of all, it had to represent the direction that America was taking at the time. Airplanes were entering the jet age, washing machines were automatic, and televisions were sitting in most every living room in America. Indeed, America was on a new path, a path that led to a new and brighter future. Aerodynamics would play an important role in taking America to that new future, and the automobile would come to resemble the jet as well.

America was obsessed with the need to go fast. As the age of the jet began to unfold during the 1950s, the quest for speed took on unheard-of proportions. The crossover from piston power to jet propulsion redefined the science of aerodynamics. A close examination of the tail section of

Pontiac used a sculpted masterpiece on the 1957 Bonneville. Heavy use of chrome and a sweeping fin spoke of America's passion for the jet age.

Lockheed's P-38 Lightning shows the beginning indications of a wind-cheating fin, while a modern F-16 is the culmination of that slippery design. Perhaps it was inevitable that automobile design would mimic the aircraft designs of the day. There

In stark contrast to the fin design of 1948, Cadillac's fin for 1960 was a sleek and slender design that was an aerodynamic masterpiece. Through the years the fin saw several different modifications with extensive use of chrome and many variations of taillight themes that stretched the imagination. Again, the fin was taking its cue from the aviation industry as man's quest to go higher and faster resulted in new dimensions in aircraft design.

This is the fin that started it all. Harley Earl's design of the 1948 Cadillac set in motion a styling theme that would last for the next decade. The inspiration for the new design came from Lockheed's P-38 Lightning, which used a number of Cadillac components in its Allison V-1710 engine. Automobile design would continue to be influenced by aviation as the decade of the 1950s witnessed the dawning of the jet age.

By 1963, the fin was finally winding down as evidenced by Studebaker's 1963 Grand Turismo Hawk. The Hawk's fin was a tasteful addition to its overall well-balanced design. While interest in the fin began to wane, the horsepower wars were beginning to evolve as Studebaker offered an R-2 engine package featuring a supercharger. Horsepower was rated at 289 and the Hawk became a serious competitor on the streets.

can be no doubt that the advent of the fin in American automobile styling caused a sensation that has yet to be equaled. Simply put, when we think of the 1950s, we think of fins. While the swept-back wing of the F-86 Sabre may have helped make optimum use of its jet engine, it is highly doubtful that any fin could help a 1959 Cadillac go any faster than its V-8 engine could propel it. No, it wasn't a matter of necessity; it was simply an exercise in the excess of design. However, before the

decade of the 1950s was over, the automobile builders in Detroit would be grafting fins onto cars that would put a fighter jet to shame. While it may have been an excessive use of sheet metal, the automobiles of the 1950s that live in the hearts and minds of people are some of the most sought after collector cars today.

Perhaps it was no accident that the design team at Cadillac constructed a small but noticeable fin on the rear quarter of the 1948 Cadillac. After all, the North American F-86 Sabre had just taken to the skies on October 1, 1947. With its sleek

Chevrolet introduced an all-new body for 1955. The new lineup carried a rather conservative fin that would give way to a sharper jetlike appearance by 1957. Chevrolet offered a number of variations based on its new design including a sedan, hardtop, convertible, and a two-door wagon that was known as the Nomad. All carried the unique tailfin treatment that would propel Chevrolet through the decade of the 1950s and beyond.

fuselage and swept-back wings, the F-86 gave a strong indication of the future of aviation, but less apparent was the impact that Cadillac's design would have on the automobile. What started as a simple concession to the world of aerodynamics would ultimately end in some of the wildest car designs ever to roll out of Detroit. The little bump on the rear fenders of the late 1940s Cadillacs would remain dormant and almost unnoticeable

well into the early 1950s, when it slowly began to grow into an intricate part of the body. The design work from the Art & Colour Section at General Motors headed by Harley Earl signaled to the rest of Detroit that a change was in the air.

It wouldn't take long for others to catch on, and soon the rest of Detroit would be sprouting fins of their own. Although GM would lead the way for several years, the mid-1950s would see challenges from all of the other manufacturers. Not to be outdone, the Chrysler division mirrored GM's development beginning with the 1955 line-up. Although its bolted-on fin looked more like a home for its taillight than a true fin, it did add to the rear fender's height and length. The Mopar folks knew they were onto something good, and the fin became a major design feature for 1956. By 1957, Chrysler left no doubt that they were a main contender in the fin wars. The battle lines were drawn, and others would also join in the frenzy. By the time it was over, the 1960 Plymouth Belvedere and Fury would have fins that could only be called vertical stabilizers. Tasteful? Maybe not, but they never fail to turn heads at the local car show.

Not one to be left out, Ford saw a vision of its future with the 1949 lineup. A slight lateral bulge in the upper rear fender seemed to grow a little each year. By 1952, the taillight was conspiciously housed in its own jetlike pod that protruded slightly from the rear. For 1955, the beautiful Crown Victoria featured a bladelike fin that ran its entire rear quarter. The stylish Thunderbird also made its debut in 1955, but in a move that could only have been planned obsolescence, its rear fender treatment was somewhat docile. The Thunderbird's fin would grow throughout the 1950s, but so would the car itself. By 1957, the Fairlane would hold a long fin that started with a sweeping curve at the midbody. Ford would use this design feature very

Buick created the beautiful Skylark for 1953. It was pure luxury through and through. While Buick would create some of the most radical fins ever during the late 1950s, the tasteful 1953 Skylark used a thicker fin that housed its taillights in two separate pods. Note that the fin's width is still rather wide. In the following years, height would increase while width would decrease, creating a sharper fin.

tastefully during the 1950s, and, like Chrysler, its fin wouldn't reach aircraft proportions until the size of the automobile demanded more of the fin.

Many independent car manufacturers continued to thrive in the early 1950s, but as the struggle to survive became harder for the little guys, the design concession of the fin would cause many to scramble for the funds involved in new tooling. As Nash merged with Hudson to create American

Motors, a new design for 1958 revealed the unmistakable fin that ran its rear length. A slight change for 1959 revealed a sleeker fin, but a true fin nonetheless. By 1961, the fin was a mere shadow of its former self with only a slight outcropping protruding from the car's rear quarter panel, and in 1962, it was gone altogether.

While Studebaker's merger with Packard in 1954 was something that most Packard purists would choose to forget, it did give both companies a few more years of life in a crowded market. Strangely enough, Studebaker chose to mimic the lower portion of the new jets rather than the upper. A close look at a 1948 Studebaker reveals a taillight that looks more like an exhaust port of a jet rather than a simple taillight assembly. Studebaker would remain docile with its rear fender treatment for a number of years, but would ultimately explode with the 1956 Champion. There was no doubt about it, Studebaker was in the game, and although they wouldn't play for very long, they would produce some stylish cars.

The 1950s would produce the wonderful fin. It was a phenomenon that would know no boundaries. Not only would the leaders use the fin, but also the struggling independents. All of the various divisions would additionally fall into line as Pontiac, Mercury, and DeSoto also sported lateral stabilizers at some point. That the automotive world was left with such a wonderful array of automobiles from this era is truly to the benefit of all. To many it was a time of growth, to others it was a time of innocence, but to car enthusiasts everywhere it was a fascinating exploration of style. The automobile of the 1950s made a statement, and that statement was that length was good, height was better, and loud was OK. Join us as we take a look at the fin and trace its evolution from a humble little sprout to an aerodynamic piece of history.

Beginnings of the Fin

M any historians have long believed that the tooling of America's war machines for World War II was perhaps the greatest industrial effort in history. Factories that once manufactured everything from children's toys to automobiles were turned into munitions suppliers overnight. In order to assist in the war effort, great automobile companies such as General Motors, Ford, Nash, Packard, and Chrysler would build everything from tanks to bombers. While the war machine raged, Americans kept themselves on wheels by keeping their old

Packard introduced its Twenty-Sixth Series on November 21, 1952. Styling was crisp and clean while the chrome accent strips on the rear quarters gave an indication of the future. By 1958, Packard's last year of production, the fin had grown into a taller vertical sweep that was an intricate part of the body. The demise of Packard was seen as a great loss to the American automobile community. Automobile Quarterly

109

The new 1948 Series 62 Cadillac was even better with the top down, ready for a drive in the country. After several years of manufacturing battle tanks for World War II, Cadillac unveiled its first new postwar offering on the Series 61, 62, and Fleetwood Sixty Special. Cadillac engine components powered Lockheed's P-38 Lightning, one of America's premier fighter planes for the war. Cadillac also built the M-5 light tank, and later the heavier and more powerful M-24 for the U.S. Army during World War II.

machines running. This involved some serious innovation on the part of many car owners as the struggle to get around became harder and harder during the war years. Used parts were sold at a premium and used car prices rocketed skyward, forcing many to find transportation in the ordinary bicycle.

When the war ended in the summer of 1945, automobile builders faced a car market consisting of many elements that were previously unseen in the automotive industry. An unquenchable thirst for new cars coupled with a mass return of the nation's GIs created a demand for new cars that would take several years to fill.

Add to this the fact that many returning soldiers had pockets full of cash just itching to be spent, and one can begin to see the foundation for a new breed of cars. All of these elements meant that America was ready for a new day. After many years of conservation because of the war effort, America was eager for a little luxury. No longer would gas be rationed, and a new set of tires was only a few dollars away. Homes became more spacious and television sets were in most American households. Yes, the war was over and it was time to celebrate.

When the new-model Cadillac hit the streets in 1948, there was one very noticeable styling characteristic that set it apart from all of the rest. Its long and smooth body was accented by two small humps on top of the rear quarter panels. Conservative Cadillac dealers were aghast when they saw them, but the negative opinions were quickly put to rest when the general public greeted

Kaiser was one of the first to offer a completely new postwar style. While the 1947 introductory model would carry the traditionally rounded prewar lines, improvements would come with the 1951 model. The addition of a chrome spear on the upper rear quarter gave the impression of a small fin. Sadly, Kaiser would not live to see the end of the fin wars as the company would cease production in the United States in 1955. This Kaiser Carolina is one of only 308 built in 1953.

them favorably. How did they get there? The answer to that has several versions.

The practical use of the fin had been around for some time prior to its commercialization by Cadillac in 1948. Many land-speed-record cars had made use of the fin in their attempts to stabilize the automobile at high speeds. Giovanni Savonucci, an Italian designer, had also made fins a prominent feature on his Italian Cisitalia in 1947. The fin's influence in American automobile design can be traced to Cadillac, although exactly who was responsible for it is a matter of which version the reader subscribes to.

One version is that during a 113-day strike at GM, Cadillac designer Frank Hershey invited the Cadillac design group out to his farm just north of Detriot to continue working on a new concept for the 1948 Cadillac. During this time Harley Earl often drove out in his own automobile, the Y-Job, to check out the progress on the concept. When

In keeping with America's love affair with high-powered aircraft, Kaiser chose a jet-inspired hood ornament that gave no indication of the lack of power beneath the hood. Power for the Kaiser Carolina came from a 226.2-cubic-inch inline-six rated at 118 horsepower. The Carolina was the bottom of the line for Kaiser while the top was the Dragon. In stark contrast to the Carolina, the Dragon was a lavishly appointed automobile that even featured gold-plated trim.

Ford's tasteful use of the fin for 1953 looked right at home on the elegant Country Squire. The simple design made only a mention of things to come. Ford's fin would grow a little each year until it occupied a substantial portion of the rear quarter panel. This particular wagon has been treated to a full restoration and now plies the country roads with ease.

the strike ended, Hershey went back to the studio and grafted the developing fins onto the full-size clay model of the 1948 Cadillac. Cadillac General Manager Nick Dreystadt and even Harley Earl didn't care for the fin at first, but GM President Charles E. Wilson thought that the fins gave Cadillac a good identity and helped to separate the marque from the other GM divisions.

Another version of the fin's origin, and perhaps the most accurate one, is that GM stylists Frank Hershey and Ned Nickles were working on the concept at Hershey's special projects studio. Hershey had a tailfin on his concept design for GM's British Vauxhall in 1944. Yet another version tells of Bill Mitchell, Cadillac design stylist, returning from the military in 1945 and introducing a tailfin design for the new Cadillac. Perhaps the most exciting version of the fin is the legend of Harley Earl's design team and the P-38 Lightning.

Prior to World War II, Earl sent a group of stylists from his Art & Colour Section out to Selfridge Field near Detroit to take a look at the new

Elegant use of a woodgrain appliqué added a significant touch of class to the Country Squire. As the decade wore on, the fin would find its way onto everything from convertibles to station wagons.

created from the drawings. Work would have continued uninterrupted except for the Japanese attack on Pearl Harbor on December 7, 1941, which completely altered the course of any new car development. All of Detroit would spend the next several years in service of the government. While this would detract from the progression of the automobile's design, its impact on the automobile's future would become evident in the postwar era.

Cadillac, like all other car builders, spent the war years focusing on war materials. The Cadillac V-8 engine was the weapon of choice for the company's new M-5 tank, which was built for the U.S. Army. Cadillac's most important contribution to the war effort was hardly its well-engineered war products, but rather the astounding speed with which it was able to convert to war production. It took only 55 days for the first M-5 tank to roll off the assembly line at its Clark Avenue assembly plant. It was the first of many tanks, and while it is doubtful that the tanks influenced the design of the tailfin, Cadillac's contribution to the war effort advanced its standing with the American public to a new level. The people who built Cadillac's tanks took great pride in their work, and the men who fought in them had no trouble remembering that their lives had been saved by those incredible tanks when they returned home from the war. Perhaps it was no coincidence that Cadillac built many of the components for the Allison aircraft engine that powered the P-38. The plane that had inspired the fins on the 1948 Cadillac was actually powered by components from Cadillac. When Harley Earl's team took the P-38 tailfin treatment and grafted it onto the 1948 Cadillac, the circle was complete.

Less than two months after Cadillac ended production of the M-42 tank, a brand-new Series 62 four-door sedan was driven off the assembly line on October 17, 1945. It was little more than a

top-secret Lockheed P-38 Lightning. The P-38 was an unconventional airplane to say the least. Its twin Allison V-1710 engines cranked out 1,475 horsepower, but its real innovations were found in its twin fuselage design. Two long, slender tail booms complete with side-mounted air scoops were capped off at the ends by two rounded vertical stabilizers. The design was sleek and Earl's crew came away favorably impressed with the fluid lines of America's new fighter plane.

Once back in the studio, the artists began a series of sketches that would foretell the cars of the future. The wild lines of the P-38 were drawn in all sorts of dream-style creations. From the stylists' point of view, cars were easy to build on paper. Several drawings were looked upon favorably by Earl, and the P-38–inspired design features were then taken to the next step. A series of 3/8-scale models, known as the "Interceptor" series, were

Power for the Country Squire came from Ford's flathead V-8. Horsepower was rated at 110 and the flathead had proven itself a fearsome competitor on the street and on the track. Many racing enthusiasts were partial to the flathead due to its reliability and performance. This flathead V-8 pulls the Country Squire with ease.

warmed-over 1942 model, but it was Cadillac's first new car in three years. Cadillac would build only 1,142 cars in 1945 against standing orders for more than 100,000 cars. The intense effort required to fill orders left little time for the development of a new model and it would be 1948 before Cadillac would offer a new look.

With the war finally over, the race was on to supply the nation with new cars. The only real new car was from Kaiser-Frazer, which offered the nation a new and dramatic automobile. Kaiser-Frazer would experience some degree of success in its beginning years, but would ultimately fall as

the competition caught up. Cadillac would merely pick up where it had left off, and after two years a new design was ready. It made its debut on the Series 61, 62, and Fleetwood Sixty Special. The public did not know the new style as "tailfins" just yet, but the new Cadillacs were a big hit. Conservative Cadillac advertising called the new sensation "rudder type styling." Although it is highly doubtful that any rudder could help the 4,000-pound Cadillacs steer any better, it did help the new style look longer and lower. Harley Earl had a never-ending quest to lower the automobile's profile so that its sleek and sexy lines would display

Even though the independents tried to compete, in the end it proved to be too much. Nash touted its Airflyte design as an alternative to the growing popularity of the fin, but as history shows, the fin would win in the long run. Although stylish in its own way, the 1951 Nash Rambler was still trying to shake the rounded lines of the immediate postwar era. It would take some years, but Nash would eventually develop its own version of the 1950s icon known as the fin.

better. Simply put, Earl thought that the automobile looked best when hugging the ground. These were attributes that he exploited quite successfully on his own personal cars, known as the Buick Y-Job and the LeSabre.

Cadillac's new styling sensation took the nation by storm simply because no one else had it. Those two little rudders planted the seed of a new generation of automobiles. All other postwar designs were caught off-guard. While Cadillac was pursuing its rudder-type styling theme, the independents looked on with worry. Packard continued its prewar design when the 21st series cars were introduced to a favorably impressed public.

Packard would introduce a raised rear quarter panel on its 1951 models, thus entering the fin wars. The style of the day for the independents would become known as the "bathtub" look, due to their obvious similarities to an overturned bathtub. Hudson, Nash, and Studebaker did not possess the working capital for extensive retooling, but were forced to do just that in order to keep up. Taking the bathtub look to the extreme, Nash revealed its all-new postwar design in 1949 with the Airflyte series. Streamlining was the key to the new Nash body style, although in the opinion of many, it occurred at the expense of genuine good looks.

Defining the ultimate in Buick luxury, the 1953 Roadmaster Skylark sport convertible commemorated Buick's 50th anniversary. The Skylark was built on the Roadmaster chassis, but used its own fenders with open wheelhouses that were painted in red or white. Its fin treatment was a tasteful exercise in design, as it had not yet reached gargantuan proportions. All of that would change when the 1958 models were introduced to a public that accepted nothing less than a tailfin that literally looked like a jet.

Of the Big Three, Ford was perhaps the most tasteful in its use of the tailfin. The tradition-minded folks at Ford chose a more conservative approach and their fin designs never reached a proportion that exceeded the car's lines. Ford can be credited with grafting fins onto the rear quarters in a way that was always a pleasant addition to the car. For 1946, Ford used its warmed-over prewar design with some freshening of the front grille work. It would be 1949 before Ford would show some hint of the things to

The direction of the American automobile was clearly evident in many aspects of the Skylark's design. A rocket-inspired theme graced the hood with extensive use of chrome. In a few short years the nation would head for the stars with the flight of a Jupiter rocket in December 1958. Just as the tailfin would grow to unheard-of proportions, hood ornaments would mimic the jet age and space travel as well. The Skylark's hood ornament is no exception.

In typical 1950s fashion, the interior of the 1953 Skylark was a rich assortment of leather and chrome. Buick spared no expense in building the Skylark, which sold new for $5,000. Only 1,690 Skylarks were built for 1953.

come. While Cadillac's "rudder type styling" took a vertical theme, Ford chose a slight bump on the horizontal plane for its new look. While it was little more than a leadoff point for the taillights, Ford did expand on its use. By 1951, it had become a long molding that now was taking up quite a bit of space on the rear quarter panel. When Ford redesigned its lineup in 1952, its rear quarter treatment had a definite vertical styling theme that ended in a round taillight set in a pod that was an integral part of its flowing lines. Ford remained somewhat docile with its fin treatment until 1955 when the rounded lines would give way to more linear vertical design.

Chrysler would end up being the latecomer to the dance. As late as 1952, Chrysler's designs were still void of any hint of the fin. Chrysler would bow in 1953 with a more linear design that gave a small indication of fin design. Virgil Exner was never a man to design in excess, and perhaps he was just testing the waters by adding the chrome fin to the rear quarter of the 1955 lineup. Although Chrysler was late to begin its fin treatment, its 1957 lineup would prove to be a sleek design that would set the pace for many to follow. While it took Chrysler some time to catch up with their body design, they were leading the way in the

The New Yorker featured eight chrome teeth just above the horizontal molding on the rear quarter, which would go on to become a hallmark on the New Yorker for years to come. Chrysler manufactured only 921 New Yorker convertibles for 1956. It was a beautiful car that was favored among those with a few extra dollars to spend. The New Yorker convertible sold new for $4,136.

The heart of the New Yorker was Chrysler's famous Hemi V-8. Cubic inch displacement was increased to 354 in 1956. Horsepower also increased to 280 for the New Yorker, but paled in comparison to the 300B, which cranked out 340 horsepower. Chrysler Hemis would go on to rule the streets during the musclecar era. Although the New Yorker was a powerful automobile, it represented Chrysler luxury at its best.

horsepower race. The letter-series Chryslers were some of the most powerful cars of their day.

World War II had a definite impact on the design of the American automobile, and many of those innovations can be directly traced to the building of faster and better airplanes. Among them was the North American F-86 Sabre, the first jet to enter service for the U.S. Air Force. While the P-38 gave rise to the general fin idea, the F-86 took it to new heights. The F-86 featured lines that were unheard of

in the piston aircraft era. All of its surfaces were swept back to a slippery 35 degrees. Despite being somewhat underpowered, the Sabre's design enabled it to surpass the piston aircrafts' speed with ease. No doubt this fact was not lost on Detroit's car builders, and even if the Sabre's speed wasn't blinding, it looked fast even when it was parked on the tarmac. Just as the Sabre took aircraft design to a new level, the tailfin would do the same for the American automobile. After building faster and better jets, America

Chevrolet introduced a new body for 1955. Riding on a 115-inch wheelbase, the new look was greeted favorably by the general public. The top-of-the-line Bel Air Series featured richly upholstered interiors, chrome spears both fore and aft, and full wheel covers. Power came from Chevrolet's 265-cubic-inch V-8 rated at 162 horsepower. With the 1955 lineup, Chevrolet literally crossed the line into the sleeker and sexier 1950s. Gone were the rounded lines of the immediate postwar era and in came the new linear look that would go on to define the decade.

would become obsessed with space travel, adding yet another chapter to the era of fins.

It would take some time for the idea to catch on, but when it did Detroit simply went wild with the fin. No other styling characteristic would play such a remarkable role in automotive design. Detroit built it, and America loved it. By the mid-1950s, it was clearly evident that something was in the air. As we shall see in the next chapter the fin was taking root, and as America entered the decade of innocence the fin would become a more important aspect to the automobile's design than the engine that made it go. Americans couldn't get enough of that so-called "vertical stabilizer."

In the beginning, it all came back to Cadillac's rudder-type styling. Many automotive historians have often said that Harley Earl's talent was not in the design itself, but was often in the ability to pick the design that the general public would like. To this end, Earl was a master at gauging public opinion. His selection of the two little rudders for the 1948 Cadillac set in motion a styling theme that would take command of the decade to follow. The rudders would grow a little each year until an all-out battle broke out between the car builders for the biggest fin of all. Before it was over, America would be left with some of the finest cars that ever graced the streets.

Chevrolet's fins looked at home with the top up or down on the 1955 Bel Air convertible. The new style proved to be a winner as many motorists bought new Chevys in 1955. Chevrolet would update this design for a few more years until a major restyling in 1958 would add length and weight to the Chevy lineup.

The Idea
Catches On

As the American public began to notice the ever-increasing length of the automobile during the early 1950s, the fin began to show signs that it was here to stay, at least for a while. Some were starting to demonstrate the growth that would define the fin movement, but most were still built to house the aviation-inspired taillights that were quickly gaining acceptance. What had started as a simple design concession to the aviation

Although the Corvette began its life with a fin-styled taillight pod, styling for 1956 saw the tailfin completely eliminated. The 1954 on the left featured the classic introductory Corvette design, while the 1958 model on the right clearly indicates the Corvette's future. In response to Ford's new Thunderbird, the Corvette received V-8 power in 1955, but it still wasn't enough as the T-Bird's production of 16,155 cars eclipsed the Corvette's production figure of 700.

Cadillac's restyle for 1950 still featured the small P-38–inspired tailfins that defined the infancy of the fin movement. Overall, automobile design was becoming longer and lower, and by the mid-1950s it would change completely as the modern postwar look took over. Cadillac would sell over 100,000 cars for 1950, which clearly demonstrated the fin's growing popularity.

Ford introduced the Thunderbird in 1955 to a motoring public that was swept away by the cute little two-seater. In a shot aimed directly at the Corvette, Ford would sell 16,155 Thunderbirds in the car's introductory year. The tasteful use of chrome and a tiny, but noticeable fin were only a small part of the Thunderbird's appeal. Power for the new Thunderbird was from a 292-cubic-inch V-8 that made the T-Bird a lively performer.

industry was quickly becoming a popular item in American car design. Fins were well on their way to growing up, out, and in any direction that would make the rear quarter look more aerodynamic. Anyone with an eye for style knew that something was going on, and that something was the noticeable growth of the fin as it took hold of the motoring public. Those that had entered the fin craze by merely adding on a bolted chrome trim piece now

had cause to retool with an integrated fin design. The public knew the real McCoy when they saw it, and a bolt-on fin just wouldn't do.

The industry fin leader Cadillac restyled in 1950, and although there were changes in front-end design as well as major trim upgrades, the small P-38–inspired tail treatment still reigned supreme on the rear quarter. The new 1950 Cadillac had a generally longer and lower appearance

Ford reintroduced the Continental in 1956 and although it was clearly a beautiful automobile, it lacked the huge fin that was becoming all the rage in the mid-1950s. Ford spared no expense in the Continental, and each one was delivered to the dealer in a fleece-lined canvas bag. A lofty price tag in the $10,000 range put the Continental out of reach of the average buyer, and the Continental Mark II would be phased out after only two years in production.

that was accented by sweeping lines on the entire body. The European racing circuit was aghast when American sportsman Briggs Cunningham entered two 1950 Cadillacs in the 24 Hours of Le Mans in 1950. Although one of the racers carried a relatively stock body, the other was an aerodynamic thoroughbred racer. The car was appropriately dubbed *"Le Monstre"* (The Monster) due to its massive size when compared to the nimble European road racers of the day. Cunningham's cars would

finish a respectable 10th and 11th thanks in part to Cadillac's 331-cubic-inch V-8.

The new lineup for Cadillac in 1950 saw the company quickly shedding its immediate postwar design and moving into the wonderful 1950s with lightning speed. If there was any doubt as to the fin's growing popularity, it was put to rest in 1950 when for the first time in its 48-year history, Cadillac sold more than 100,000 cars. Cadillac would celebrate its Golden Anniversary in 1952 with only

Pontiac featured a completely redesigned body for 1955 that spoke directly to the "more is better" theme of the 1950s. A huge divided bumper up front and twin "Silver Streak" bands set Pontiac apart from the competition. Wraparound windshields were also new for 1955 and made a significant contribution to the new streamlined look. Although the tailfin was still small, the stage was now set for the explosion of the large tailfin that would signify the 1950s.

a minor face-lift, but the P-38–inspired tailfins were still an intricate part of the Cadillac look. The P-38 inspiration would be seen all the way into 1956, but as evidenced by the Eldorado in 1955, Cadillac's fin would play a much more important role for the 1957 lineup.

The one aspect of automobile design that GM designer Harley Earl aimed for was a clear identity among the different makes. This accounts for some of the design features found on GM's postwar lineup. Pontiac featured an Indian-head hood ornament, while Cadillac carried a chrome V on the

129

Pontiac's Silver Streak styling theme carried through the entire length of the car ending with an elegant tailfin that gave a slight hint of things to come. GM's use of two-tone colors again made for an attractive automobile that the public loved. Pontiac would rank sixth in the industry with a calendar year production of 581,860 units.

Although the design for Plymouth's 1955 lineup was already in place, a last-minute change by Chrysler stylist Virgil Exner resulted in a car that was right at home in the mid-1950s. The new design by Exner allowed Plymouth to cross the line into the modern postwar look of the 1950s with ease. The wild tailfin treatment was only a few short years away, and Plymouth would be ready. Plymouth produced 8,473 Belvedere convertibles like the one pictured here.

hood and deck lid. There were also signature rocket-shaped taillight lenses and a streamlined, aerodynamic, jet-inspired hood ornament found on the Oldsmobile. A fascinating story lies behind the porthole treatment that was a mainstay of Buick for many years. It seems that the head of Buick's design studio, Ned Nickles, was convinced by Joe Funk, one of his modelers, to try something unique on his new 1948 Buick Roadmaster Convertible. Funk cut three holes in the Buick's front fenders, then installed lights that flashed in synchronization with the spark plugs. The effect was mesmerizing, and when Buick's Executive Vice President Harlow Curtice noticed the cutouts, he insisted that the

design become standard on the 1949 Buick. The dies were retooled and the final result was the signature portholes that became Buick's most recognizable feature for many years to come.

This was the way things were done in the styling studios of the day. In an age long before the advent of computer-aided design, cars were designed by a simple method involving the human hand, a hand often dried out from working with clay or stiff from holding a pencil. There was also the input of many talented people, but the process had a pecking order that defined what the ultimate design would be. At GM, if Harley Earl didn't like it, it was unlikely to become a final design.

Plymouth's tailfin treatment for 1955 was sheer beauty in motion. A linear edge that ran the car's length culminated in a large oval pod that housed the taillight. The whole package resulted in a smooth design that the motoring public loved. Two-tone color treatments added to the appeal of Plymouth's offerings for 1955.

Dodge jumped into the fin wars with both feet in 1956. Although the 1956 Dodge lineup was largely a carryover from the previous year, a big, beautiful tailfin became an intricate part of the rear quarter panel. Dodge was also nursing the beginning of the musclecar era with a multitude of V-8 engines available up to 295 horsepower. Dodge would win 11 NASCAR events in 1956, proving that horsepower was a serious issue. Push-button automatic shifting was also a big hit, and Dodge would post a production of 233,686 cars for the model year.

Although many designers were rubbing their chins in the early and mid-1950s, conservative styling still stood as the hallmark of Ford's lineup. The introduction of the Thunderbird in 1955 gave the public an impressive look into the new idea of an American sports car. Although it was initially billed as such, many Europeans balked at the idea of an American sports car. No, it may not have handled like the Jaguar XK 140, but it looked great and featured a 292-cubic-inch V-8 that propelled the 2,980-pound T-Bird with ease. While Ford was certainly aware of the fins' gaining popularity during the early 1950s, they chose the theme of planned obsolescence as the introductory Thunderbird fea-

While Dodge placed a heavy emphasis on horsepower for 1956, there was no doubt that the company was in the fin wars for good. Dodge's fins had grown taller and more aerodynamic and left little doubt as to the company's intentions. Fin treatment was one of the few upgrades for Dodge in 1956 as strong sales in 1955 called for only a minor face-lift.

The 1953 model year would be Oldsmobile's last body style to carry the immediate postwar look. The Series 98 Holiday two-door hardtop was an attractive automobile that proved very popular with the motoring public. Its small but protruding tailfin was accented by chrome and ended with a rocket-inspired taillight. The Holiday Hardtop was a heavy car at 3,906 pounds, but power from its 303-cubic-inch V-8 was more than enough to move it along. Oldsmobile captured nine NASCAR events in 1953.

tured a low-keyed rear quarter treatment that was both stylish and tasteful. While its competitor, the Corvette, withered on the vine for lack of sales, the Thunderbird gained unheard-of popularity and would spend the 1950s in a steady state of development that saw its fins grow just a bit each year.

In contrast, the Corvette would shed its rocket-inspired pod on the rear quarter for a smooth look on the 1956 model. The Corvette would spend the 1950s in stark defiance of the fin phenomenon and in the end would pay dearly as the Thunderbird would outsell it hands down. There were some experimental fins grafted onto the Corvette, but none of these would ever reach the production stage. Instead, the public either accepted or rejected the finless fiberglass wonder from Chevrolet. Of course the Corvette would have the last laugh as prices for the early-model Corvette have climbed astronomically in recent years.

The Corvette would not be the only automobile to attempt to defy the oncoming roar of the fin. On October 16, 1954, William Clay Ford announced that Ford had created a Continental Division and was about to release a whole new version of Edsel's original design. Although it certainly was a beautiful car, more attention was paid to maintaining the roots of the original design than to the demand for the fin. When Ford introduced the Continental Mark II in 1956, it was clearly an about-face of the accepted design practice of the day. Again, Ford can be credited with a tasteful design while maintaining supreme elegance. The

It might have been the Lockheed F-104 Starfighter or the Grumman F-9F Cougar that provided the inspiration for Oldsmobile's hood mascot, but the jetlike chrome piece mounted on the hood left little doubt as to where GM was going. The sleek chromium mascot would point the way on several Oldsmobile models over the next few years. Oldsmobile would play a prominent part in the fin wars as its designs of the late 1950s would be as wild as any that roamed the streets at the time.

A complete restyle for Oldsmobile in 1954 saw the company move into the mid-1950s with a clear vision of the future. A new longer and lower look set the stage for the coming fin wars. Its fin remained little more than a taillight pod, but it still carried its jet plane hood mascot up front. Oldsmobile's new crisp and clean styling helped the company capture fourth place in industry output with a total of 433,810 units for the calendar year.

company also went to great lengths to ensure that the Mark II had no equal in terms of quality and craftsmanship. Each engine was dynamometer-tested and then torn down for inspection before installation. All bolts used in its assembly were of aircraft grade, and all wheel and tire assemblies were precision-balanced by hand. The Mark II was shipped to dealers in a fleece-lined canvas bag. While it was a hit at the Paris Auto Show when introduced on October 6, 1955, its design was most definitely

Although Cadillac's 1956 Eldorado featured a fin signifying the company's future designs, the Coupe DeVille still carried the P-38–inspired tailfin from 1948. Cadillac's cars had grown longer and heavier, but their smooth and graceful lines were right at home in the mid-1950s. Nineteen fifty-six would be the last year of the original fin design as all Cadillacs would be accented with a new longer and taller fin design for the coming year. The stage was now set for the very pinnacle of the fin's dominance in American car design.

acting in defiance of the accepted practice of the day. No wild fin treatment, no excessive use of chrome, and a lofty price tag in the $10,000 range put the Mark II in a league of its own. In a clear demonstration of the fin's popularity, the Mark II would bow out after only two years of production. Ford would produce a mere 2,996 Mark IIs, and in an ironic twist of fate the Oakland Boulevard

assembly plant that built the Mark II would retool for production of the new Edsel. Lincoln would completely restyle with the Mark III in 1958 and it would bear little resemblance to the Continental Mark II.

Many car builders were still using a conservative approach to the fin in the mid-1950s. While many were still developing their new designs in the early 1950s, hostilities overseas again began to cause a ripple effect on the American car market. When the North Korean army invaded South Korea on June 25, 1950, many already knew that it was just a matter of time before the conflict spread. With the fate of the free world once again at stake, the United States again found itself in a war against communism. The war effort demanded new and better munitions, and the U.S. government turned to Detroit as the United States again began tooling up for the war effort. While its size and scope would not reach the proportions of World War II, the retooling did have an impact on Detroit. Cadillac continued to build tanks while many other car builders built various other components for the conflict.

Although the war siphoned off some of Detroit's industrial capacity, it also gave impetus for the development of a new generation of jet-powered aircraft. This new generation of jets would prove to be inspirational in the design of the American automobile. Of course, developmental work on jet-powered aircraft had taken place for some time, but the Korean War proved that the United States needed a fast and agile fighter plane. This need gave rise to a new breed of sleek jets that had one thing in common, a more aerodynamic design than anything the world had previously seen. This slippery new look would not be lost in Detroit as the tailfin and many other trim pieces began to resemble some of this new breed of aircraft. Jets such as the Lockheed F-80 Shooting Star and the F-94 Starfire were inspirational in the new look of the automobile. With power measured in terms of thrust and speeds reaching previously unheard-of proportions, the jet age was proving to be the driving force in American car design. Of course there were other indirect factors driving American aviation efforts during the early 1950s,

not the least of which was the Soviet Union's introduction of the MiG-9. This early jet-powered fighter caused great concern in the U.S. Air Force, and companies such as Lockheed, North American, and Grumman scrambled to fill contracts from the U.S. government for new and better jets. Overall, the early 1950s would see an incredible effort in the development of new and better jets for the nation's defense. While the average American couldn't own one of these new jets, they could have a fender spear or a jet hood mascot on their new car.

When hostilities in Korea ended in the summer of 1953, the United States was once again at peace. With the lessons of aerodynamics learned from the steadily developing jet age, Detroit's designers could now turn their attention to the automobile. Designers such as Harley Earl and Virgil Exner began to push their designers for new and faster-looking cars that would satisfy the nation's need for speed. The direction of Cadillac's future design completely changed in 1952 when a talented young designer named Dave Holls joined Cadillac's design staff and quickly began work under the direction of Harley Earl. It was Holls who designed the ultimate finned warrior as he created the 1959 Cadillac tailfin that would serve as the defining fin of the 1950s. Holls spent his career at the design studios of General Motors and turned out some of Detroit's most fascinating automobiles.

The general growth of the fin is easily traced through marques such as Oldsmobile. As one of the original founders of the automobile itself, GM had no intention of letting its other divisions just stand by as the fin grabbed hold of the American public. For 1953, Oldsmobile offered a wonderful array of cars that clearly indicated the direction that Olds was taking. Riding on the Ninety-Eight

Chevrolet's Bel Air two-door hardtop for 1956 was a minor face-lift from the previous year, but with two-tone paint schemes and fender skirts it rode into the mid-1950s with style. Chevrolet's 1956 lineup would prove to be a winner and the company would become the nation's number one automaker with calendar-year sales of 1,621,004 units. The 1956 lineup came in a multitude of body styles with the two-door Nomad station wagon being the most expensive. The small but elegant tailfin was right at home on the 1956 lineup, but would grow even more the following year.

Series, the Holiday two-door hardtop was a handsome car that featured a long rear deck accented by two taillight pods on the rear quarter. A better indicator of the future was up front as the hood mascot was a beautiful jet-inspired chrome piece flanked by two simulated jet engines pointing the way. Oldsmobile was emphasizing its racing activities and was a favorite winner at many NASCAR tracks. Overall, Oldsmobile captured nine checkered flags at NASCAR events in 1953, including Buck Baker's win at the Southern 500. For 1954, Oldsmobile restyled and had completely shed its rounded look of the late 1940s. The tailfin was little more than a rounded pod for its taillight, but the Oldsmobile jet still stood guard on the hood. A slight restyle of the tailfin for 1956 saw the rear quarter panel receiving a more sculptured look that spoke loudly to the fin movement. Although the quintessential finned Oldsmobile was still a few model years away, a close look at Oldsmobile's designs in the preceding years of the late 1950s shows how the fin was creeping up and crawling into the hearts of the American motorist.

As Chrysler entered the 1950s, a movement was under way in the company to build smaller cars. This was in response to several marketing surveys that said the public wanted smaller cars. The marketing people must have had to look hard for people who wanted these cars since this was certainly not the case. As Chrysler entered the 1953 model year, both Plymouth and Dodge had shed an average of 670 pounds over the previous year. They were also visually smaller than the traditional Ford, Pontiac, or Chevrolet. The downsizing resulted in the loss of a substantial portion of Chrysler's market share. Clearly, something had to be done. The answer came from the legendary Virgil Exner, who in the space of 18 months managed to redesign Chrysler's entire lineup for 1955. The result was a longer and lower car that propelled all four marques from the Chrysler camp to great success. Plymouth's 1955 Belvedere convertible featured a longer and lower body that quickly brought it up to par with the competition. Although Plymouth's fin for 1955 lacked the vertical height that would become the hallmark of fin design, it did make ideal use of a streamlined taillight, and a restyle in 1956 would see the addition of a genuine tailfin. As Dodge made clear in 1956, the folks at Mopar were not about to be left behind in the fin wars. A large, sweeping fin with

its taillights set vertically was just what the motoring public was looking for. DeSoto featured a stunning design for 1955 that proved that Mopar would not be outdone in the design department. Once again the aerodynamic, jet-inspired design was in vogue as Mopar's 1956 lineup would be very successful. As we shall see later on, Chrysler would draw a line in the sand with its 1957 models, which would turn out to be some of the most beautiful cars of the day.

With the postwar market's insatiable appetite for new automobiles quickly becoming filled, Detroit drifted into the mid-1950s with a renewed sense of competition. The independents were struggling to keep up with the well-capitalized Big Three. Although many were already on their deathbeds, there would be several efforts to defy the odds and survive. The mid-1950s would see several mergers that meant a few more years in the market for some, and certain death for others. While this struggle was a gallant one, the ranks of the car builders would thin considerably in the next decade.

By the mid-1950s, the stage was set for the explosion of the fin. Even though there was certainly an attractive look to the rounded taillight pod, Detroit would soon find out that it was not enough. The next several years witnessed a sharp increase in the fin's height as well as its length. No longer would a slight fin be grafted onto the automobile; the automobile itself would be built around the tailfin. While the public would flock to it in droves, they would also catch a glimpse of many of Detroit's dreams. As we shall see in the next chapter, the fins of the 1950s were predominant on the production automobile, but the real fin craze was found in the design studios of Detroit. Yes, the fin was here to stay, and it was about to head into outer space.

3

Detroit Goes Wild

If the general public thought that the fin was becoming excessive, one look at the New York or Chicago Auto Shows in the mid-1950s gave the consumer a strong indication that the best was yet to come. While the fin was quickly entering its renaissance period during the mid-1950s, there were many ideas locked up in Detroit's design studios that would prove that America's love affair with the fin was not over yet.

The 1956 Firebird II took a different direction from its predecessor. While it was still gas turbine–powered, it featured seating for four and was much larger than the Firebird I. Aircraft inspiration is clearly evident once again as demonstrated by the turbine-inspired air intakes up front. The Firebird II still delights crowds today as shown here on display at the 1996 Meadowbrook Concours. Don Keefe

The Cadillac La Espada was one of three custom-built show cars for the 1954 General Motors Motorama. The La Espada rode on a 115-inch wheelbase and featured a fiberglass body. The future was foretold in many of the La Espada's design features, which included a sharply raked 60-degree windshield and superfins that would show up on production-model Cadillacs in just a few years. The name "La Espada" would never find its way onto a production-based Cadillac, but its design features were a clear indication of the future. National Automotive History Collection, Detroit Public Library

Even though many dream cars would prove to be mere thoughts of fantasy, some did give rise to many interesting ideas that found their way onto the production-based cars of the day. Concept cars that carried the banner for their respective companies on the show circuit were actually built for more than just show. Many of them served as rolling test beds to gauge the public's opinion on various design features. This enabled the car builders of Detroit to effectively measure the public's opinion without endangering sales of an all-new car. While some concept cars were built for nothing more than show, many others were built only as scale model mock-ups. In any case, our study of the wonderful

fin would not be complete without taking a glimpse at Detroit's dream machines.

If dream cars are created by thought, then clay is the medium through which they are expressed. Within the safe confines of the various manufacturers' special project design studios, modelers were free to test the limits of style and taste. To be sure, most of the experimental work would never see the light of day in terms of production. After all, the American public loved something new, but there is a big difference between something different and something new. A good case in point was the introduction of the Edsel in 1958. Other than the usual teething problems associated with a new car,

Cadillac's experimental show car for 1959 was the XP-74 Cadillac Cyclone. The design influence of the fin is clearly evident, as the Cyclone seemed to be straight out of a science fiction movie. The Cyclone was built with several gadgets that dazzled the general public. The car was equipped with a power-operated rear-hinged bubble canopy that opened and closed for exit and entry. The two missile-inspired pods up front housed a proximity warning system that informed the driver of impending hazards. Note the lower skeg moldings that would later show up on the 1961 production-based Cadillac. Bud Juneau collection

there was nothing mechanically wrong with the Edsel, it merely had a new and different look. However, the "horse collar" front-end treatment was simply more than the public could take and it did not sell well. Buick also experienced sales problems when it introduced an all-new look for 1959. While it was clearly keeping pace with the fin movement, it proved to be much more than conservative Buick buyers could handle. The result was a disastrous sales year for the company. While the fin had crept into the hearts of the motoring public slowly, Ford's Edsel and Buick's new style had attempted to change the public's mind overnight.

Where does a dream car come from and how is it built? The answer to these questions lies in the hearts and minds of the designers. Men such as Virgil Exner, Harley Earl, Dick Teague, Dave Holls, and Gil Spear were men of vision who wielded a powerful pencil in the car-building industry. After all, the automobile's reliability had been proven some decades before. By the 1950s, the average American family could simply jump into the sedan and head for the open road. The need to bring along a trunk full of spare tires or engine parts had passed some years before. The nation's highways were smooth and a service sta-

The beautiful X-1000 was designed at the request of Ford's vice president and general manager of styling George Walker, shown here with a 3/8-scale model of the design. The X-1000 was designed by Ford designer Alex Tremulis at Ford's Advanced Studio during 1955–1956. Man's fascination with space travel is clearly evident as even its fins were retractable. While it certainly was interesting to look at, no body panels from the X-1000 would show up on any production-based Ford. From the Collections of Henry Ford Museum & Greenfield Village

tion was just around the corner. With dependability a proven science, the design of the automobile could now take center stage. A close look at the postwar marketing campaign of any given car builder usually reveals only passing remarks on reliability. Indeed it was the style, color, and other visual cues that attempted to sell the latest model.

So it was that Detroit would build its dream cars. These are the cars that didn't make it to the production stage, but caused a major stir on the show circuits. The sky was the limit on these special automobiles that were built not for sheer numbers, but existed only to see how far the design studios could go. Of course some components would reach the streets of America. Perhaps a headlight here or a tailfin there, but overall, dream cars allowed the public to do just that, dream. Maybe the average car buyer couldn't have the Ford FX-Atmos sitting in their driveway, but a Fairlane 500 Skyliner was certainly a possibility.

Although dream cars of the 1950s with their aircraft-styled fins and rocket nose cone front ends made everyone look twice, many were little more than mock-ups. With bodies molded of fiberglass, clay, and aluminum, dream cars were usually put together in a very short amount of time. Some

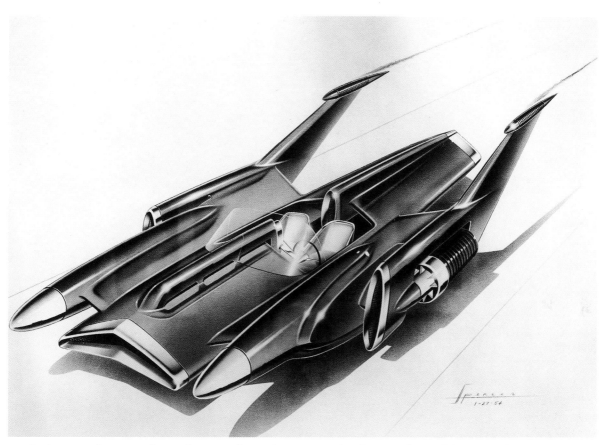

Ford's design studios were alive with energy during the 1950s and nothing was beyond the scope of the designer's pencil. This drawing of the 1954 Exploratta is an indication of just how far Ford went in the studio. Resembling more of a rocket than a car, the general public was left to decide its source of power, as turbine, electric, or nuclear were all possibilities. The Exploratta clearly defines the limits of the fin movement as the design studios of Detroit were letting their imaginations run wild during the height of the fin craze. From the Collections of Henry Ford Museum & Greenfield Village

were built without engines, leaving the general public to guess if it was going to be gas turbine–powered, electric-, or maybe even nuclear-powered. Others were built in miniature in order to see what their final form would look like. Some scale-model concept cars were even motorized with small engines and operated by radio control to enable the designers to see what they looked like while in motion. Whatever its size or power,

the dream car lived only to inspire the automotive public and it usually did just that, although only for a short time. The sad truth is that many dream cars were scrapped after serving on the tour circuit for a year or two. Some did survive and continue to delight all who are able to catch a glimpse of these incredible machines that are kept in the vaults of various museums and collections today. It is only fitting that interest in the dream

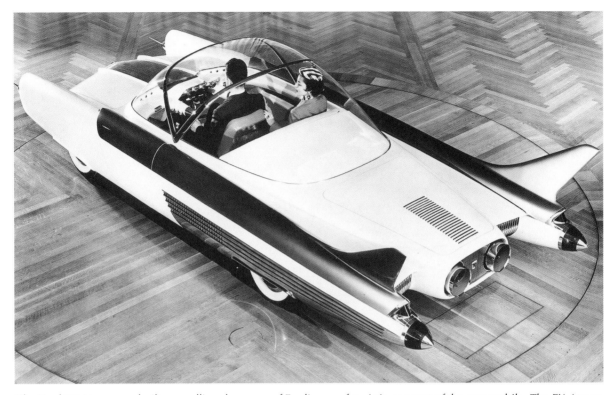

The Ford FX-Atmos was built as a rolling showcase of Ford's superfuturistic concept of the automobile. The FX-Atmos was a big hit at the 1954 Chicago Auto Show and the general public couldn't get enough of the wonderful show cars of Detroit's fancy. The FX-Atmos was built only as a fiberglass show car and had no supporting structure. Sadly, by the mid-1960s, the car began to sag and its Plexiglas roof began to discolor. It was then broken up, although a small model of the car still exists today. Note the aircraft-inspired tailfins. From the Collections of Henry Ford Museum & Greenfield Village

car concept would reach its heyday in the thick of the fin wars of the 1950s.

Credit for the dream car concept can be given to Harley Earl, whose influence and charisma wielded a considerable amount of power at General Motors. Indeed, Earl's power at GM caused many to tremble at the mention of his name. He worked long hours and demanded that everyone who worked for him do the same. Much of Earl's charisma originated from his early years spent at GM's La Salle and Cadillac divisions. GM had recruited Earl for the design of the 1927 La Salle

and his resulting effort shocked the automotive world. Never before had such stunning lines of European influence been seen on an American production-based vehicle. The 1927 La Salle put Earl's name on the map in automotive design. With his success firmly planted on his first attempt at a production vehicle, it is easy to imagine the influence he had gained at GM by the 1950s. Indeed, the legend of Harley Earl is still talked of in Detroit today. The General Motors Motorama Auto Shows enabled Earl to start his design work with a blank sheet of paper. No

The Lincoln Futura was one of the fortunate dream cars built as a running automobile. The Futura was the brainchild of Lincoln's head of styling, Bill Schmidt. The design is clearly aircraft inspired as evidenced by the twin jet–styled canopies and fins both fore and aft. Schmidt claimed that the design was also inspired by tropical sea life as evidenced by the sharklike features on the front end. The Futura would go on to achieve fame in Hollywood as the Batmobile, *created by George Barris.* From the Collections of Henry Ford Museum & Greenfield Village

longer reworks of an old design, the Motorama cars of the 1950s were outrageous and showed the public what a car could look like when crossed with a rocket.

Harley Earl and Dave Holls' work at Cadillac would give the public some eye-catching designs during the fin craze of the 1950s. One of Cadillac's first entries into the 1953 Motorama Auto Show was the LeMans. The LeMans featured many styling cues that ended up in production, including its entire front end, which would show up on Cadillac's 1954 models. The two-seater fiberglass roadster featured a hooded headlight that would find its way onto Cadillac's 1954 and 1957 production cars. The GM Motorama show of 1954 saw the introduction of Cadillac's La Espada and the

El Camino. Both of these cars were as wild and different as concept cars could be. The El Camino's rear fin would turn up on the 1955 Eldorado and that same fin would become the mainstay of Cadillac's 1958 lineup.

For 1955, Cadillac resurrected the name of Earl's famous creation, the La Salle. While introducing many innovations in automotive design, the La Salle show cars broke from the tradition of the fin and instead chose a smaller and more conservative design that seemed to defy the fin craze. The 1955 La Salle roadster rebelled against the trend of the day even more as its back end appeared to be cut off at the rear wheel. Both La Salle concept cars featured a cut-out behind the front wheel that would later show up on the Corvette.

As the last of GM's trio of gas turbine–powered cars, the Firebird III was a finned wonder that was all jet. Its tall vertical fins and twin-canopy design made it look more at home in the air than on the road. The Firebird III featured a multitude of fins adorning its entire body. All of the Firebird prototypes were featured as Motorama show cars and generated much excitement from the public. From the National Automotive History Collection, Detroit Public Library

At the height of the fin wars in 1959, Cadillac had gone ballistic with a concept car called the Cyclone. While many Motorama show cars openly carried an aircraft-inspired theme, the Cyclone borrowed its cues directly from man's quest to reach the stars. Its front end featured a pair of rocket nose cones, which housed a radar system that warned the driver of any obstacles in its path. Of course its rocket pods would have torpedoed anything in its path anyway, but it was a hit in 1959. The Cyclone's tailfin treatment was even more radical with two vertical stabilizers equaling the height of its bubble-styled canopy. The Cyclone definitely took the fin concept to the

limit, and one can only wonder what it might have looked like shooting down the streets of America.

Several show cars made it into production. The car known as the legendary American sports car is one of those that had a life after the show circuit. The Chevrolet Corvette made its public debut at the New York Auto Show in January 1953. There are many legendary stories of the Corvette's rocky start, one of which is its signature crossed-flags emblem. The Corvette's identification flags were actually changed on the night before the show. The original design featured an American flag—but someone realized that it is forbidden by law to use the American flag for promotional

Chrysler would enlist the help of Italian body builder Ghia for its contribution to the finned dream cars of the 1950s. This artist's rendering of the 1957 Chrysler Dart shows the smooth and balanced lines of the aerodynamic creation from Ghia. The Ghia's body panels were hand beaten by the superior craftsmen of Ghia at its plant in Turin, Italy. Power for the Ghia came from a 375-horsepower 300-C Hemi. Dr. Paul Sable collection

purposes. The Corvette's crossed-flag emblem was redesigned in time for the show and the rest is history. While the Corvette was introduced as a dream car, public reaction was so strong that it was rushed into production. The result was a car that leaked around its windows and quite simply didn't run very well due to the complexity of its multi-carbureted engine. Indeed the Corvette almost died a quiet death until it was saved by the most unlikely of saviors. The Ford Thunderbird's introduction in 1955 meant that GM had to continue production of the Corvette or abandon the two-seater market. While the Thunderbird outsold the Corvette in its early years, the Corvette did eventually reach a profitable status for GM.

The Corvette proved to be a wonderful inspiration for GM's show cars of the 1950s, but in stark defiance of the fin wars, its rear quarter treatment featured rounded lines that were tasteful and elegant. In 1954, Chevy introduced the Nomad to a delighted public. Its Corvette-inspired front end and two-door wagon concept featured a rocket-style pod in its fin. There was also a beautiful fastback Corvette–inspired car for 1954 called the Corvair. In keeping with the General Motors tradition, Chevrolet always tested a car's name before giving it an official design. Thus the Biscayne of 1955 and the Impala of 1956 were both hits on the Motorama show circuit. The Biscayne featured a double wrap-around windshield and concave door panels heading

Built by Ghia for Chrysler, the aerodynamic Ghia Gilda was the star of the 1955 Turin Show. The Gilda was a masterpiece in terms of its streamlined elegance. Its construction was aluminum over a steel frame and it featured such unusual styling tricks as partly concealed wheels and huge tailfins. Top speed for the Gilda was said to be 140 miles per hour. Dr. Paul Sable collection

toward the rear of the car. Strangely enough, Chevrolet's dream cars of the mid-1950s completely shunned the fin movement. Perhaps Chevrolet was already preparing itself for the ultimate demise of the fin. In any event, the XP 700 made its debut in 1958 as the personal car of Bill Mitchell, head of GM styling. This Corvette became a test bed for many innovations of the Corvette in future years. Vents, side coves, trim lines, and side pipes were all hung onto the XP 700 at one time or another. The 1958 XP 700 became such an interesting project that it was used as a show car for 1959. As the Corvette eased into the 1960s it would enjoy a strong appeal on the dream car circuit. There were several versions of what Corvette called the Mako Shark as well as testing for building the Corvette with midengine

power, but the fin would never become an intricate part of the Corvette's design.

While the design work on Ford's production-based automobiles would always carry a tasteful use of chrome and conservative fin height, the company's dream cars were some of the most outrageous Detroit would produce. Indeed, Ford's concept cars were the product of pure fantasy, as its tailfins would rival that of any fighter plane in existence at the time. While the designers at Ford were acutely aware of the fin's climbing popularity, the early 1950s found the company deeply engrossed in the development of a retractable hardtop.

The genesis of this idea actually started in 1948 when Ford Advanced Studio Stylist Gil Spear heard rumors of Buick's new 1949 Rivieria hardtop convertible. Spear thought that the Buick was marketing its new model on false advertising, as the top didn't actually retract in the true convertible sense. Back at his studio, Spear began work on a concept car that would ultimately test the retractable concept and become known as the Syrtis. The idea would be tossed around at Ford for a few years, but a model of the Syrtis would begin life based on the dimensions of the 1952 Ford. Here again man's fascination with outer space would play a significant role. Spear designed the Syrtis with a space ship theme that started at the front with a streamlined nose and ended with the telltale fins that were now influencing American car design.

By 1955, Ford's use of the fin on their production vehicles was still in its infancy, but back at the design studios the fin was reaching for the stars. Ford stylist Alex Tremulis designed the X-1000 during 1955–1956. The X-1000 was a pure flight of fancy. While many concept cars forecasted a significant design concept that would later appear on a production-based car, the X-1000 was a pure dream. The only components of the X-1000 that would see the production line were a few instrument panel knobs. A streamlined car by any standards, the X-1000 featured smooth lines and a huge set of fins that actually retracted into the body. The X-1000 was also designed to use a rear-mounted gas-turbine engine and it was campaigned extensively on the auto show circuit. A live display at the Chicago Auto Show featured several Ford modelers deeply engrossed in building a clay mock-up of the X-1000. This gave the general public a firsthand look at how the design studios actually worked.

One of Ford's more popular concept cars was the FX-Atmos. Built for the 1954 Chicago Auto Show, the FX-Atmos caused quite a stir. Its low-slung body accented by twin rocket pod nose cones and a wild fin treatment was second to none in the show car circuit. Its futuristic design spoke loudly to the space travel theme that was all the rage in the 1950s. The FX-Atmos was a true concept car as it never had an engine and was built purely for the public to look at. The FX-Atmos in its show form that the public saw was a fiberglass mock-up that was built by Creative Industries and took about three months to build. The entire body was molded in one piece as a solid unit; as such, the doors, trunk, and hood did not open. Its Plexiglas canopy was molded as a separate unit with a removable center section. In order for one to experience the interior of the FX-Atmos, the center section was removed and passengers were lifted in by a crane. The FX-Atmos earned its keep on the show circuit dazzling many who saw it. Sadly, by the mid-1960s its unsupported fiberglass body began to sag and it was destroyed.

Another winged warrior of the Ford show car phenomena was the Lincoln Futura. The Futura was the idea of Lincoln's head stylist, Bill Schmidt. The most unusual aspect of the Futura was its inspiration. While most of the dream cars were looking exclusively to the stars for their aerodynamic lines, the Futura took its cues from tropical sea life. The story goes that Schmidt was vacationing in the Bahamas in 1952 when a diving encounter with a shark gave him the inspiration for the Futura's design. The sharklike fins on the Futura are clearly evident from all angles. Nevertheless, the design influence of the jet era was also clearly evident in the Futura's futuristic body.

Lincoln selected Ghia of Italy to build the Futura and it was constructed in just three months at a cost of $75,000. It arrived in the United States just in time for the Chicago Auto Show on January 8, 1955. The Futura then toured the show circuit with stops in Detroit and New York. Its twin

Another beautiful creation from Ghia built for DeSoto was the Flight-Sweep I. An electrically operated convertible top and fully operational electric side windows were just a few of the luxuries built into the Flight-Sweep I. While many of Detroit's car builders would use their own studios, Chrysler relied heavily on Ghia for the creation of its dream cars. Dr. Paul Sable collection

canopy roof, huge jetlike tailfins, and simulated jetlike air intakes both fore and aft are the quintessential components of a 1950s show car. Even better was the fact that the Futura was one of the lucky show cars to actually be built as a running automobile. The Futura was truly a remarkable dream car that went on to lead a fascinating life. After its completion on the show circuit, the Futura

wound up in the hands of Hollywood car builder George Barris, who turned it into one of Hollywood's most famous cars, known as the *Batmobile*.

If Ford's dream cars were bordering on the outrageous, then the folks at GM were definitely going above and beyond the stratosphere. In 1954, GM introduced the Firebird I at the GM Motorama Auto Show. While its original design was never intended to become a production automobile, its name would surface on Dick Teague's rework of Chevrolet's Camaro for Pontiac in 1967. The Firebird I truly tested the design limits of the day. Resembling more of a rocket than an automobile, the Firebird I was powered by a 379-horsepower gas turbine engine. Several manufacturers would experiment with turbine power, but none would ever reach the production stage. GM would continue with the Firebird prototype design and would also build the Firebird II and the Firebird III. While the Firebird II began to resemble something that might actually reach the American public's driveway, the Firebird III headed directly to the stars. Looking more like something from a NASA launch pad, the Firebird III was as wild as a tailfin could ever get. Multiple use of the vertical stabilizer theme was evident in several places on the Firebird III. While certainly not practical, the Firebird III did introduce a few innovations that would eventually see the light of day. Cruise control, an antiskid braking system, and automatic headlamps were only a few of the features that would eventually find their way onto the regular-production automobile.

Not to be left out, Chrysler chose a different avenue in pursuit of their dream creations. In 1949 Chrysler President K. T. Keller hired Virgil Exner. While he may not have known it at the time, Keller had just solidified Chrysler's design direction for the next generation. Keller made Exner Director of Advanced Styling in his own studio that was known as Chrysler Styling. Within the solitude of his studio and without the pressure of production-car designs, Exner worked on Chrysler's dream cars. A visit from Italian coachbuilder Carrozzeria Ghia resulted in a series of dream cars that held an extensive European influence. In particular, the Ghia-built Dart of 1957 is a finned wonder of beautifully crafted lines.

Another beauty of Exner's dream car designs met with a sad fate. Completed after 15 months of intense labor at the Ghia facility, the car known as the *1956 Norseman* was loaded into the cargo hold of the *Andrea Doria*. The ship sank after a collision with the Swedish liner *Stockholm* and the beautiful Norseman was lost. Sadly, it now entertains nothing more than passing fish swimming by.

The fabulous 1950s would see some of the wildest fins to ever grace the roadways and exhibition halls. While they never reached the driveways of the American public, they allowed everyone's imagination to fly a little higher. What was the fate of these wonderful creations from Detroit's imagination? Sadly, many were destroyed after their useful display years were played out. Some were saved and these wonderful artifacts are among the most treasured possessions of the museums and collections that house them. The automobile has served a number of purposes over the years, but the concept cars were not built to haul around the family or make the neighborhood milk deliveries; they existed only to test and entertain our imaginations. To be certain, Detroit has not abandoned the concept car theory, but the wild fins and groundbreaking ideas of the 1950s have given way to computer-generated images of what the automobile might be like in the future. The concept car of the 1950s, with its obvious use of the infant jet-age style and tailfins that reached for the stars, remains locked in a time of innocence and grandeur.

4

Battle Lines are Drawn

As the late 1950s emerged, design and style were reaching a new level of influence in manufacturing. Everything from the automobile to the toaster was taking on a completely new look, which spoke of streamlined elegance and often gave the impression of movement while sitting still. This design feature was mainly the result of the nation's quest for speed as the aviation industry continued to make great strides in aircraft design.

Representing one of Cadillac's best for 1959, the beautiful Eldorado Biarritz convertible featured vast amounts of chrome and a powerful 345-horsepower V-8 engine that propelled the 5,060-pound finned wonder with ease. Americans looking for fuel economy would have to look elsewhere, as the 1959 Cadillac was built for beauty and style. Cadillac would assemble 142,272 cars in 1959, dominating the U.S. luxury car market.

A competitor in name only, the Imperial was a quality-built automobile that spared no expense in comfort. Riding on a huge 129-inch wheelbase, the Imperial was well suited for a night on the town. Sharp styling with finely sculptured lines made the Imperial a standout in the crowd. Quality control was a hallmark of the Imperial's image as each car was checked and rechecked for fit and finish. Despite its beauty and luxury, its rival Cadillac would outsell the Imperial by a wide margin.

America was also becoming infatuated with space exploration. The jet engine and the rocket were redefining the science of aerodynamics and this research would not be lost in Detroit's design of the automobile.

At the forefront of streamlined aircraft design work were companies such as Lockheed and Grumman. As the nation's premier builders of the new generation of jet-powered aircraft, these companies knew how to build a sleek and slippery design that

seemed to defy the laws of gravity. The Lockheed F-104 Starfighter, under development since 1952, proved itself when it entered service in 1958. The F-104 was a needle-nosed aircraft that was able to attain a level speed of 1,400 miles per hour, and climb to 15.15 miles in about 4.5 minutes. The press dubbed the F-104 "the missile with a man in it." When the first production Grumman F-9F Cougar took to the skies on January 18, 1954, its Pratt & Whitney J48-P-8 turbojet engine was pushing

Representing the top of the line for DeSoto in 1959, the Adventurer convertible featured a wide array of trim features that literally defined the 1950s. DeSoto's triple taillight theme was an outstanding example of the classic fin design that was so prominent in the 1950s. DeSoto would build only 97 Adventurer convertibles for 1959, making this example a truly rare automobile. Heavy use of gold anodizing made the Adventurer shine.

out 8,500 pounds of thrust. The F-9F's top speed of 705 miles per hour was unheard of in a piston-powered aircraft, but these were the days of the jet engine. While the general public could only dream of such blinding speeds, they could get the feel and look of the modern jet with any one of the aviation-inspired creations from Detroit.

As automobile design entered the late 1950s, it was clearly evident that everyone had caught on to industry leader Cadillac's fin; however, Cadillac

was still showing everyone the path to follow. The 1948 model with its P-38 aircraft–inspired tailfin had set a precedent that Cadillac had cultivated into complete success. Beginning in the mid-1950s, Cadillac raised the bar just a bit each year until its fins gave the impression of flight. Cadillac easily maintained its status as a trendsetter because of the ever-thinning car market of the late 1950s. The once mighty Packard was operating on life support, and Lincoln was still trying to figure things

Full-size Fords for 1959 utilized a tasteful design of the fin that was graceful and stylish. A focused effort on building a production model with a fully retractable hardtop roof had paid off with a novelty that no one else had. In a time of excess and chrome overload, Ford can be credited with using tasteful restraint in its use of the fin. Production-line Fords would never see the gargantuan proportions of the competition, but Ford's design studios would know no limits in their use of the fin.

out after dropping the Continental Mark II. The Lincoln Mark III would join its sister models the Capri and Premier and offer a fin with a long, sweeping body that would bear no resemblance whatsoever to its predecessor. Chrysler's Imperial, while proclaiming the last word in luxury and quality, was not catching on with the general public. In fact, production numbers for the Imperial didn't even come close to Cadillac. This allowed Cadillac to enter the golden era of the fin unchallenged in its command of the luxury car market. With the competition searching for its place, Cadillac took bold steps in its fin design. The rules were simple: big cars with as much chrome as the engine could pull and a tailfin that was as tall as the body would hold. While this may not sound like an exercise in

Perhaps no more beautiful than in its convertible body style, the 1957 Chevrolet Bel Air was right at home in the 1950s. Powered by Chevrolet's 265-cubic-inch V-8, the Bel Air was a spirited performer. The 1957 convertible would go on to become one of the most popular postwar collector cars in the world. Today, the 1957 Bel Air convertible commands a premium on the collector market that many would have thought impossible at its introduction. This example has been completely restored.

taste, the cars that originated from the very pinnacle of the fin era are some of the most wonderful designs to ever grace the roadways.

In 1957, Cadillac introduced a variant of one of its show cars that would impress the motoring public, especially those with money to burn. The Eldorado Brougham was based on Cadillac's 1955 Eldorado Brougham show car and featured

advanced aircraft styling. Cadillac left no stone unturned in outfitting the Eldorado Brougham in luxurious comfort, which accounted for its whopping price of $13,000. Cadillac's fin had now grown immensely from its original 1948 design, but due to the length and lower profile of Cadillac's late-1950s style, its fin looked right at home. The general public loved the 1957 Cadillacs and

The sharp dorsal fin on the 1957 Chevrolet would prove to be a classic design that would represent one of the most memorable milestones of the fin era. Chevrolet produced this fin design for one year only as 1958 would bring a complete change. Chevrolet outsold its rival Ford by a mere 136 cars in the calendar year 1957, marking one of the closest races ever in the quest to be number one.

After grooming the fin for several years, Oldsmobile Introduced a jet-like fin in 1958. The Super 88 convertible was a heavy car weighing in at 4,217 pounds. Power came from Oldsmobile's 371-cubic-inch V-8 that generated 305 horsepower. Oldsmobile was in firm command of the medium-price-class market in 1958 and many buyers found good value in Oldsmobile. Sadly, the marque has now been added to the casualty list in the ever-thinning car market of the new millennium. Bud Juneau

the numbers proved it. Cadillac would sell 146,841 cars in 1957, placing the company ninth in industry sales for the second year in a row.

Cadillac's 1958 lineup was generally a carry-over from 1957. There were a few minor changes and the Brougham's interior received a bit more attention, but overall Cadillac chose to let the success of its cars sell themselves. While Cadillac's fins were selling well, its power up front was propelling the huge cars with ease. Cadillac's standard engine for 1958 was the 365-cubic-inch V-8,

which generated 310 horsepower. With a little more modification, the same V-8 pumped out 355 horsepower through the use of a triple carburetor setup. The message was clear: Cadillac's cars were big, they were long, and, in spite of their size, they were fast.

The absolute king of the fin wars made its debut in 1959. Cadillac introduced the 1959 lineup to a motoring public that thought they had seen it all. An excessive but tasteful use of sheet metal made Cadillac's 1959 lineup everything that a 1950s car

A forlorn 1958 Chevrolet Biscayne looks right at home parked on Main Street U.S.A. Styling for Chevrolet took a left turn for 1958, and a larger and more rounded body saw a reduction of the fin's height. It was now slanted and held two taillights mounted horizontally. Although completely restyled, Chevrolet's 1958 lineup proved immensely popular with the motoring public. Over 1,217,047 Chevrolets were built in the model year.

could be. Its long and sharp tailfin featured two bullet-inspired taillamps that seemed to want to take the car into flight. This quintessential design, which truly demonstrates the ultimate fin of the 1950s, was the design work of noted General Motors design stylist Dave Holls. Holls' double-bullet fin on the 1959 Cadillac has come to represent the entire movement of the fin during the 1950s. If we can credit Harley Earl with starting the fin movement, then we can also credit Holls with taking it to the limit, and also with winding it down in such a way

that it went out with respect. The design of the 1959 Cadillac proved that a tall vertical stabilizer could have a home on a car that couldn't fly. Series 75 Cadillacs rode on a long 149.75-inch wheelbase, while the rest of the lineup used a 130-inch wheelbase. These were not small cars as their extensive use of chrome and breathtaking length were bold designs that spoke of Cadillac's dominance of the fin wars. To be sure, everyone else had their own idea of what the fin should look like, but Cadillac remained in a class all its own.

A new body greeted Chevrolet buyers for 1959, and the fins were once again a prominent part of the new design. A horizontal gull-wing theme and matching cat-eye taillamps made the 1959 lineup a standout in the crowd. This two-door Impala Sport Coupe has been treated to a complete restoration. The Chevrolet Impala and the rest of Chevrolet's lineup proved to be very popular with the public and the GM division built 1,481,071 cars for the model year.

Chrysler had gained a strong foothold in the fin wars by 1956, and with Virgil Exner's "100-million-dollar look" in firm control, the company entered the height of the fin craze with full force. Styling for 1957 was absolutely beautiful as Chrysler took the prestigious *Motor Trend* "Car of the Year" award. Not only were Chrysler's cars illuminating the parking lots of the local country club, but they were also burning up the pavement thanks

to the letter-series cars. Starting in 1955, Chrysler offered the 300 Series cars with power as the main theme. For 1957, Chrysler offered the 300 C convertible, of which only 484 were built. Those that have survived are now commanding premium prices on the collector market. The 300 C had it all: good looks, comfortable interior, and power to spare. The 300 C came with a 392-cubic-inch V-8 that was carbureted with not one, but two four-barrel Carters

Buick was dubbed "The Year's Most Changed Car" when the company introduced an all-new style for 1959. In an attempt to literally change the company's image, old model names were dropped and the new names LeSabre, Invicta, and Electra were now carrying the Buick banner. The bold new style proved to be more than conservative Buick buyers could handle and Buick's sales ranking in the market dropped to a postwar low.

that enabled the big V-8 to crank out an astounding 375 horsepower. Fin design for the 300 C was tall and sweeping across the entire rear length of the car. Chrysler had truly captured the look of the fin without disgracing its original intent. Of premier concern to Chrysler was the comfort of its passengers as the company even offered the optional "Highway HiFi," which allowed the occupants to play their records while traveling the roadways of America.

Luxury as defined by Chrysler in 1958 came in the form of the Imperial. Advertised as "America's most distinctive fine car," the Imperial left no stone unturned when it came to quality and refinement. The Imperial was big with a wheelbase of 129 inches (149.5 for the Crown Imperial) and weighed in at close to 5,000 pounds depending on body style. The Imperial carried a tasteful fin that was set apart from the competition by the use of a circular gun sight–type design that was truly elegant.

Quality control for the Imperial was a major factor in every car built. According to historical records, as many as 17 hours were spent on each car just to ensure that the doors fit perfectly.

When Plymouth introduced its 1958 lineup on October 16, 1957, there was a subtle difference in the fin's height. Plymouth was not apprehensive about maintaining its place in the fin wars. After placing third in American automobile sales in 1957, the company had no intention of relinquishing its place in the market. Crisp, clean, and attractive styling gave the customers just what they wanted. Unfortunately, 1958 would prove to be a recession year for the auto industry with American automobile sales down 22 percent. Despite Plymouth's 34 percent loss in sales, the company still maintained its third-place standing in the market. Plymouth's streamlined styling was clearly evident in the Belvedere two-door hardtop. Riding on a 118-inch wheelbase, the Belvedere featured a 317.6-cubic-inch V-8 that propelled the 3,410-pound car with ease. There was also a subseries on the Belvedere line called the Fury, which came only in a two-door sport coupe and featured a tweaked engine that managed a respectable 290 horsepower. A wonderful array of two-tone body colors

Virgil Exner's work for Chrysler during the 1950s took the company's design work to higher standards. Chrysler caught onto the fin idea relatively early in the game, and by 1957, it had fins that were riding with the best. The powerful 1957 300C was a car of stunning beauty, and it was a lively performer. Detroit was just beginning to cultivate the musclecar phenomenon that would reach its height in the 1960s.

Pontiac introduced the beautiful Bonneville for 1957. Availability was limited to one per dealer for the stylish Bonneville, which contained a number of design features that indicated Pontiac's direction for the coming years. Fuel injection was featured on the Bonneville, of which only 630 were built for the year. There was no shortage of bright work on Pontiac's wonderful creation, which helped sell the rest of the line. Pontiac would be the nation's sixth-largest automobile builder in 1957.

enhanced Plymouth's appeal. There was certainly no doubt that Plymouth was in the thick of the fin wars, and would go to great lengths to keep up with the competition.

Another Chrysler division, DeSoto, made good use of its sheet metal by building the Adventurer. The Adventurer was DeSoto's top-of-the-line offering for 1959, and it was in a class all by itself. A triple-taillight fin set it apart from everything else on the road. The Adventurer, a car of stunning elegance, was also a lively performer thanks to its 383-cubic-inch V-8 that used two four-barrel

carburetors. DeSoto would build only 97 Adventurer convertibles for 1959, making it a very rare car in today's collector market. Extensive use of gold anodized trim on the rear quarter panels gave a look of true elegance.

While Ford's stylists were building some of the most far-out designs ever seen in the styling studios, production Fords continued the tradition of restrained elegance for the late 1950s. For 1957, the Thunderbird received a face-lift that lengthened the rear of the car. Fins now played a prominent part on the Thunderbird, although they were

In a design that could only have come from the aviation industry, the 1957 Bonneville made no attempt to hide its jet-styled inspiration. The entire assembly mimicked the jet age in every way. Pontiac proved that the height of the fin didn't necessarily have to be tall in order to garner attention. The extensive use of chrome and stainless steel said it all.

The Pontiac Safari wagon was a classy way to haul the American family around. Plenty of upper-line trim appointments made the Safari a wonderful way to hit the open road for the family vacation. This 1957 Star Chief Custom Safari two-door wagon has already achieved Milestone status.

still relatively small when compared to the competition. Nevertheless, the fin treatment on Ford's 1957 Thunderbird proved to be a wonderful design, as the company would build 21,380 Thunderbirds for the motoring public. Ford's 1957 Thunderbird would turn out to be the last of the two-seaters. Nineteen fifty-eight saw the Thunderbird grow into a four-seater that changed the personality of the Thunderbird forever.

Full-size Fords also benefited from the designers' use of restrained elegance, as Ford would outproduce rival Chevrolet to become America's number one automobile producer for the 1957 model year. The big news for 1957 was the addition of the Skyliner. The Skyliner was a convertible hardtop that featured a completely disappearing roof. What amazed the public even more was that all of this happened with the touch of a button. Because

For 1958, Pontiac's Bonneville received a new body that was as smooth and graceful as any car of the fin era. Power was still a major theme with Pontiac, as the Bonneville would use a 370-cubic-inch engine that generated 285 horsepower. Two-tone color treatments made for an attractive package in the Bonneville lineup.

the mechanism was a complex series of servos and relays, it was truly an impressive sight. The retractable roof was interesting to say the least, but a restoration of one of Ford's complex Skyliners is a challenge that most would shy away from.

By the height of the fin wars in 1959, Ford's lineup again proved that less was better. As the American public gobbled up anything with wings on the rear quarters, Ford chose a classic design that earned the company a Gold Medal for Exceptional Styling at the Brussels World Fair. Ford's

stark defiance of the superfin craze of 1959 was a brave undertaking. In the face of the competition, Ford proved that good taste could still be found in the simplistic design of an automobile. In 1960, Ford would redesign its fin and it would become a mere horizontal slant on the rear deck. To credit Ford's design studios, Ford certainly had the resources and the design inspiration to build fins with the rest of Detroit, but for the most part the company chose to remain on the sidelines of the fin wars.

The Pontiac Bonneville's mimicking of the jet age took matters one step further for 1958 and used a jetlike air intake on its rear quarter just aft of the door. The half-cylinder set off by an upper and lower trim sweep was an inspirational trim piece that spoke directly to the aviation theme of the day.

If Ford was showing restraint in its use of the fin, rival Chevrolet was more than making up for it in their 1957 lineup. Chevrolet grafted a huge fin onto the 1957s that would go on to become an icon of the classic fin era. Changes for Chevrolet were clearly evident as a new front bumper made its debut. Chevrolet made good use of a gold anodized finish on the grille work up front, and redesigned headlight assemblies containing air

intakes for the interior made for a beautiful, yet functional, front end. The hood featured two menacing rocket-inspired pods that directly reflected the aeronautic theme of the day. Chevrolet would offer three series for 1957 with body trim appointments signifying the difference between the One-Fifty, Two-Ten, and the Bel Air. No matter what the buyer was able to afford, all models came with those wonderful fins. In a neat styling trick that fooled many gas-station attendants, Chevrolet hid the fuel filler cap behind the chrome housing on the rear of the left fin. Chevrolet's beautiful design for 1957 was a hit on any model, but perhaps is best displayed on the Bel Air convertible. In what would be a very close race, Chevrolet would build only 144 more cars than Ford in 1957, but Ford would beat Chevrolet in model year production, thus making Ford the nation's number one automobile builder. Once again, Ford's restrained design proved popular with the motoring public.

For 1958, Chevrolet would take a side road in terms of its fin development and actually tone down the fin's height and sharpness. Gone was the sharklike dorsal fin that sat so predominately on the 1957s, and in its place was a rounded fin that featured two taillights set horizontally apart from one another. While most of Detroit was operating on the two-year plan—where a new body style was introduced every two years with a face-lift in between—Chevrolet had been face-lifting its line-up for the past three years. The 1958 models represented the last of Harley Earl's reign at GM, and Bill Mitchell would now lead GM's styling. The 1958s would prove to be a one-year wonder, as 1959 would see the introduction of a universal body that brought GM, and the fin, back in line. Chevrolet's lineup for 1959 featured a sleek new body that was definitely at home in the late 1950s. A new tailfin design that resembled a gull-wing

Rambler's Ambassador was well appointed for 1958 and featured a sharp fin on the rear. Rambler would be the only car company to increase sales in the recession year of 1958. The Ambassador was a lively performer, thanks to its 327-cubic-inch V-8 rated at 270 horsepower. Rambler would cross over into the 1960s with the guidance of company president George Romney, and would prove to be very successful in the coming years.

affair was very attractive on the low-slung body. Chevrolet's fin for 1959 was literally laid over horizontally in a design that was different from any fin yet seen. Clearly, the era of the large rounded lines inspired by Harley Earl had passed.

Another GM division, Buick, was also all new for 1959. In an attempt to change its image, Buick even changed the names of its models for 1959. Gone was the low-end Special, replaced by the name LeSabre. The midlevel Buick previously known as the Century now carried the name Invicta, and the top-of-the-line model was now known as the Electra and Electra 225, replacing the Super and the Roadmaster. Everything about the new Buick was a radical departure from Buick's traditional sense of styling. The new Buick was longer, lower, and wider. Headlights were set at an angle, as were the fins on the rear. Simple bullet-nosed taillights sat below the huge fins. Buick advertised that these cars didn't even look like Buicks, and the

Even radio antennas were not safe from the aviation-inspired designs of the day. Rambler's Ambassador featured an antenna that was mounted in the middle of the trunk and was swept back to imitate the dorsal fin of one of the many jets of the era. Plenty of chrome set the Ambassador apart from the rest of Rambler's offerings for 1958.

general public agreed. The new style proved to be more than traditional Buick buyers could handle and sales dropped to a postwar low. Although they were not a hit with the public when introduced, the 1959 Buicks with their huge diagonal tailfins are a true representation of the late-1950s fin.

Not to be left out in the cold, Pontiac was sporting some of the most beautiful cars ever to roll out of Detroit during the late 1950s. In 1957, Pontiac aimed its marketing plans directly at the younger generation. The infamous Silver Streak styling theme that had been a mainstay at Pontiac for so many years was removed. In a move that set Pontiac apart from all of the rest, Pontiac's fin would not be the big feature in the car's design, but rather its adornment of trim work would be its claim to fame, even though Pontiac's fin would be absolutely jetlike in its appearance. It is rumored that one owner of a 1957 Pontiac noted that children would not stand near the rear of the car for fear of being burned by the jet blast. Side spear treatments and a multitude of color schemes set Pontiac apart from the competition. All new for 1957 was the limited-run Bonneville, which came only in a fuel-injected convertible. At $5,782, the Bonneville was the most expensive Pontiac by far and only 630 Bonnevilles were built for 1957, which makes them very rare in today's collector market.

Another offering from Pontiac was the Safari wagon. Luxurious appointments again set the Safari apart from the competition. As a two-door wagon, the Safari introduced the American family to a sporty way to take the all-important summer vacation. Safaris were powered by Pontiac's 347-cubic-inch V-8, making them lively performers as well. If there was any doubt that the trim-laden Pontiacs were inspired by the aviation industry, they were quickly put to rest when the 1958 Pontiac Bonneville hit the streets. In a move that must have been borrowed from Lockheed's Starfighter jet, the 1958 Bonneville featured a jetlike air intake pod that sat just aft of the doors. Fins were redesigned for 1958, and they now sat horizontally with two taillights housed in the rear pod. Overall, the late 1950s would see wonderful cars from the Pontiac division.

Packard and Studebaker had also jumped in with both feet as fins were an intricate part of each car's design. One of the last of the independents, Rambler was still fighting for survival in the thick of the fin wars, but made great strides during the late 1950s. After a merger that saw the marriage of Nash-Kelvinator, and Hudson became known as American Motors Corporation, the company made the decision to drop the Nash and Hudson names for 1958. Instead they would concentrate on selling a revised series of cars and a newer version of the original Rambler compact car. While the Rambler American was completely devoid of the fin, it did offer economy at a good price, which was something that the American public warmed up to in the recession year of 1958. Those who wanted Rambler's quality with a set of fins could choose

from any of Rambler's other offerings. The company would boast a sales increase in the recession year of 1958 and would be the only automobile company to do so as all others declined in sales. Rambler had the good fortune of having the right car at the right time.

The years 1957 through 1959 proved to be the very pinnacle of fin design for the American automobile. Longer and lower bodies mated to large-horsepower engines were the order of the day. Never before and never again would the motoring public have the chance to buy such wonderful cars. As America crossed over into the 1960s, the fin would begin to diminish and the nation would forever leave the decade of innocence. Yes, it was almost over, but some of Detroit's car builders still had a few tricks up their sleeves.

Cadillac's new design for 1959 would prove to be the absolute pinnacle for fin design of the 1950s. Longer and lower bodies accented by an extreme fin that housed twin bullet-like taillights was an attractive style that the public loved. The 1959 Cadillacs had a wheelbase of 149.75 inches on the Series 75, and 130 inches on the remaining models. The flowing lines of the two-door hardtop made the Coupe DeVille look even longer than it actually was. This example is finshed in Kensington Green.

5

Winding Down

By 1960, the fin had begun to play itself out. As with any fad, the general public's interest in the fin began to wane. America was now entering the decade of the 1960s, and the age of innocence was beginning to slip away. Although Americans did not yet realize it, they were about to enter a decade of turmoil. Over the course of the next several years the nation would be shattered by a missile crisis, the assassination of an American president, and U.S. entrance into a war from which there

After several years of contention in the fin wars, Mercury chose a look of simplicity for its top-of-the-line 1960 Park Lane. The rear bumper housed a dramatic taillight lens that featured extreme vertical height and was accented by a tastefully curved fin. Mercury chose to keep the fin alive for a few more years despite the fact that most others were eliminating it by the early 1960s. A small fin could be seen on Mercury's lineup into the 1963 model year.

Cadillac introduced a simplified and more elegant automobile for 1960. The company that had literally invented the chrome-accented wonders of the 1950s was now shedding the "more is better" theme in favor of sheer beauty. The twin bullet lights of 1959 were replaced by a streamlined lens that was mounted on the trailing edge of its bladed fin. The Eldorado Seville two-door hardtop was especially elegant in Cadillac's hue of Champagne with an Olympic White Vicodec fabric roof.

would be no easy return. The decade of the 1950s was gone, but the fin would remain a factor in several of Detroit's designs.

After the design-shattering statement made by the fin, it was almost impossible to just eliminate it overnight. Instead, most car manufacturers chose to decrease the fin's visual impact a little each year until it was completely eliminated on most cars by the mid-1960s. Many car manufacturers crossed into the decade with a new design causing vast changes to the fin. Conservative styling began to reign supreme, and many marques drastically reduced the amount of chrome on their new offerings as well. Although the fin would soldier on for a few more years, gone were the days when bigger was better. American Motors had proven that there was room in the market for a finless economy car in 1958 with the Rambler American, and more Americans began to recognize the cost-saving measures of a smaller car. The dinosaur-sized cruiser of the

For 1961, Cadillac offered some major styling changes that had been previewed on the 1959 and 1960 Eldorado Broughams. The bodies were wonderfully sculptured with sweeping horizontal lines that featured a full-length lower-body skeg that matched the upper fin at the rear quarter. The lower skeg fin had been previewed on the 1959 Cyclone show car. A minor recession in 1961 resulted in a total production run of 138,379 cars against 1960's total of 142,184. The most visual change in the rear was the taillight treatment, which now ran horizontally just above the bumper. This 1961 Coupe DeVille is finished in Laredo Tan.

1950s was on its way to extinction, but it wouldn't die with a bang. Instead it would slowly creep out of style just as gracefully as it had crept in.

Luxury car leader Cadillac made extensive changes for 1960. Gone was the double bullet taillights mounted on the fin and in was a new sharply bladed appendage. The look that had ruled 1959 was now a victim of the past. Cadillac's fin was now a sleek and streamlined design that took Cadillac to new highs in terms of elegant simplicity. A new full-width grille coupled with a noticeable reduction in the amount of trim made for a more conservative styling statement. The new Cadillacs were more elegant in their "less is more" theme for 1960, but Cadillac's fin would begin its steady decline from this point forward.

A restyled Cadillac greeted buyers in 1961. Cadillac continued to tone down its offerings by making a concession to the economy market, something that the general public wasn't ready to accept in the nation's premier luxury car. A new Short Deck Sedan was introduced in the Series 62 lineup. The new Short Deck Sedan was a full 7 inches shorter than other production-model Cadillacs.

Chevrolet's 1960 Impala continued the use of a gull-wing–type fin that made for an attractive and classic look. A linear design that saw an upper trim line extend all the way back to the rear fin was aerodynamic and slippery. An aircraft-inspired side trim treatment proved that space exploration and aviation were still major factors in American automobile design. Chevrolet's fin for 1960 is displayed nicely on this Impala convertible finished in Roman Red.

Buyers rejected the shortened Series 62 and in the end only 3,756 were built. Competition for Cadillac's 1961 lineup included an all-new design of the Lincoln Continental that included a four-door convertible. The Lincoln's design was stunning, and despite the fact that fins were not a prominent feature, it is recognized today as one of the most outstanding automobiles to ever grace the roadways.

Chevrolet introduced a face-lift on its 1960 lineup and made only slight changes to its models. The graceful swanlike fins from 1959 now had a more angular look and the cat's-eye rear taillights were replaced by a more traditional lens that was set in a beauty panel. The gorgeous wraparound windshield continued for 1960, and styling was especially classy on the two-door hardtop and convertible. Chevrolet's lineup for 1961 saw its fin reduced to a mere ridge line running across the rear quarter and rounding the rear deck, and a restyle in 1962 saw the fin disappear from Chevrolet's models forever. The company that had produced the classically finned Bel Air from 1957 was now marching headlong into the musclecar era with its Super Sport and Corvette models. The

After a dismal sales year in 1959, Buick chose to face-lift its body in hopes of winning back traditional Buick buyers. A new look for 1960 was achieved by rounding the bodylines and sculpturing the sides for an effect that was pleasing from any angle. In an attempt to bring traditional Buick buyers back into the showrooms, ventiports were reintroduced for 1960. Buick still retained its new model names with the LeSabre, Invicta, Electra, and Electra 225 carrying the Buick banner for 1960.

company's focus had changed, and the fin was no longer a design factor in Chevrolet's lineup.

The writing was also on the wall at Buick where lessons learned from the previous year were hard at work. Buick continued to share many components with several of its GM counterparts, but the 1960 design was more than just a face-lift. In order to increase sales, Buick knew that it could

not rely on the previous year's design, which proved to be disastrous in terms of the public's acceptance. Buick's fin was thus toned down, clipped, and rounded while the sides and front received a little more artwork in the form of sculptured bodylines. Ventiports returned in 1960, most likely in an ill-fated attempt to lure back some of the more traditional Buick buyers. In the end the

Buick's fin was toned down for 1960, and a more rounded look now reigned. The angle of Buick's fin was still sharp, and it still carried a look of elegance from the rear. The conservative refinements would not help, as Buick would slip even further down the industry sales ladder. Nevertheless, Buick's Invicta was a well-balanced design that remains a big hit at the local car shows today.

Pontiac drastically altered its fin for 1960 by reducing its visual height and trim work. After years of excessive amounts of chrome and body styles that spoke directly to the aviation movement of the 1950s, Pontiac would cross into the 1960s with a look that gave a strong indication of GM's direction in the near future. Pontiac was quickly shedding its stodgy postwar image and focusing on performance. In a few short years the musclecar movement would begin to awaken, giving birth to such legendary cars as the GTO and Firebird.

face-lift didn't work, as Buick would sell fewer cars in 1960 than during its postwar low in 1959. In fact, Buick would produce 253,999 cars for the model year in 1960, earning it a ninth-place ranking in industry sales. This was Buick's lowest ranking in the industry since 1905. Although they were not a big hit when new, the modern collector market has recognized the 1959 and 1960 Buicks as one of the premier cruisers of the fin era. Buick would spend the decade of the 1960s redefining itself as a

performance car builder and would go on to produce the Wildcat and the Riviera in an attempt to entice younger buyers. The fin would quietly leave Buick in 1961.

The year 1960 would mark another restyle for Pontiac. The only body component that did not change was the roof. A new hood, grille, and sculptured fender all came together at a point to form a front end that was sharp and attractive. On the rear, Pontiac would be one of Detroit's first to

Plymouth chose to carry its extreme vertical fin into 1960 as the Savoy clearly demonstrates. The extremely tall appendage was in stark contrast to the competition, which was now reducing the overall height of the fin. Plymouth did have the foresight to carry the Valiant as a concession to the growing economy market. Plymouth would also restyle in 1961, and its fin would pass into history, as a flat deck would grace the rear of all full-size Plymouths.

completely abandon the vertical appeal of the tailfin. Instead, the rear taillights were held in two rather simplistic pods that made no attempt to be the focal point of the car. Overall, Pontiac chose the theme of simplicity, form, and function for 1960. Pontiac would spend the 1960s concentrating on the musclecar as the wonderful Grand Prix, GTO, and Firebird would go on to burn up the streets of America. Pontiac had entered a new age, and the book was now closed on Pontiac's era of the fin.

One of the few car manufacturers that continued to offer a large fin into the 1960 model year was Plymouth. While others were toning down

their use of the fin, Plymouth's huge dorsal fin continued to resemble the jets that inspired it. Plymouth had an eye on the future when it marketed the Valiant line for Chrysler in 1960 as a concession to the growing movement toward economy. The Valiant proved to be very successful due to its economical price. The rest of the Plymouth line received a rework of its front-end sheet metal that used an unusual side cove treatment just ahead of the front wheels. While this would be Plymouth's last year of the fin, it wouldn't just drift out as others had done. Plymouth would literally cross from 1960 to 1961 by completely eliminating the fin. In a demonstration of Plymouth's extended use of the

The 1961 model year would be the last of Virgil Exner's fin design at Chrysler. Chrysler's fin had now gained a look of elegance, and its trailing edge was a sharply angled affair that fit nicely on the finely sculptured lines of its cars. The fins adorning this Newport Town & Country wagon finished in Sahara Tan add a look of refinement that was the crowning end of Exner's contribution to the fin wars.

now-waning fin, Rambler would move into third place for 1960, pushing Plymouth into forth.

As with everyone else, Chrysler also toned down the fin as it crossed into the new decade. For 1960, Chrysler featured a restyled body with a fin that was slightly altered for the new model. The tailfin design was lengthened for 1961, and this would be the last year that Virgil Exner gave input into the fin's design. The man who had led Chrysler through the era of finned elegance was now entering the latter part of his exciting career. Exner would remain a Chrysler consultant until 1964, and he remained active by starting his own private industrial design firm with his son. Exner passed away on December 22, 1973, and with his passing came the end of an era in automotive design history.

While most car builders were scrambling for new designs that signaled the end of the fin, Ford would have no trouble reducing the height of its fin due to the fact that its fin had never reached astronomical proportions. In particular, Mercury usually employed tasteful styling tactics, and their graceful exit from the 1950s would showcase a linear design that crossed into the new decade of the 1960s with a classic look. After experimenting with several different versions of the fin in the late 1950s, Mercury decided that it had enough. A straight and simple line, beginning at the rear door edge and extending back to its large oval taillight,

By 1962, Mercury had erased most of the fins on the Monterey although there was still a slight rise on the rear quarter panel. The small fin ended with a circular pod that housed the taillight. The overall appearance of the Monterey clearly demonstrated the direction of Mercury for the decade of the 1960s. Strangely enough, Mercury would resurrect a fin for 1963 on the Monterey, and its Comet and Meteor line still carried a small fin until 1963.

DeSoto's last stand came in 1961, as the once proud marque would cease production in November of 1960. This beautiful 1961 DeSoto is finished in Mediterranean Blue and has a mere 35,000 miles on the odometer. DeSoto still represented good value for the money in 1961, and power came from a 361-cubic-inch V-8 that featured 265 horsepower. Note the extreme lateral length of DeSoto's last fin; it begins at the front door and extends all the way back to the rear deck.

had its formerly proud fin slumping over in a curved fashion. The look was fresh and didn't detract from the overall appearance of Mercury's cars for 1960. For 1962, Mercury's fin was still prevalent in its Comet model, but the Monterey's fin treatment was merely a small lateral hump that housed a single taillamp at the rear. To be fair, Mercury kept a small hint of the fin alive for several years after the bubble burst, but it would never again see the vertical height of the late 1950s.

A sad note would mar the beginning of the decade as the once proud DeSoto would pass into history. After years of providing solid transportation

to the American motoring public, DeSoto would cease to exist on November 30, 1960. The recession year of 1958 was not kind to DeSoto, which saw a 60 percent decline in production. DeSoto limped through its last few years as many had already predicted the demise of the marque. The last DeSotos produced would bear close resemblance to their Chrysler counterparts, with a slightly reworked fin for its last year. There were many who mourned the passing of the DeSoto, but its memory is kept alive today by numerous enthusiasts who gain gratification from owning a car that's a little unusual. DeSoto's contribution to the

The angled look of DeSoto's fin for 1961 was in stark contrast to the tall vertical standing fin of 1959. In a clear demonstration of the fin's refinement over the years, it had grown up and out, but had finally come to rest at an angle. The fin had truly made its mark in the course of American car design. Note the absence of excessive chrome and linear influence on the surrounding brightwork.

fin wars of the late 1950s certainly should not be underestimated. Fins were a dominant design feature for DeSoto during the height of the fin craze, and its triple taillight theme still reigns supreme as a hallmark in the entire fin movement.

The 1960s would also claim another great automobile, as Studebaker would not see the end of the decade. After turning out cars for generations of Americans, Studebaker's luck in the crowded 1960s market wouldn't last long. Studebaker fared well in the immediate postwar market when automobile-starved Americans bought anything on

wheels, but as the tide changed in favor of the buyers in the early 1950s, Studebaker began to feel the pressure of a crowded car market. A merger with Packard in 1954 was not enough to stem the flow of red ink, but Studebaker would survive through the 1950s and would produce some stylish cars. Studebaker was also a prominent player in the fin wars with cars such as the Hawk. Studebaker took a cue from Rambler and introduced the economy-minded Lark in 1959. The Lark would help the company through the lean times. Studebaker tried hard to survive in the car market, but in the end the company was outgunned by the big players in the automobile industry. The company that had started by making horse-drawn wagons in 1852 closed its doors in 1966.

The last traditional fin for the American car can be credited to Cadillac. As the company that began the entire movement back in 1948, it was only fitting that it would lead the fin movement out. Cadillac's design for 1964 featured a small fin that was a mere shadow of its former self. The once proud vertical stabilizer that been a hallmark of Cadillac's design for so many years was now just a sharply contoured appendage to the rear quarter that still

managed to project a proud connection to its past. By now the general public had grown weary of the fin and it no longer had a place as a prominent feature in American car design. The next year, 1965, would see the end of the once glorious fin, as the new models featured all-new finless styling. Cadillac's rear quarter design would feature sharp vertical lines for several more years, but the traditional vertical fin was now gone. A chapter in Cadillac's history that had literally defined its dominance of the luxury car market had come to a close.

The tailfin left as quietly as it had entered the American automobile scene. While they are

Famed designer Brooks Stevens was contracted to rework Studebaker's Hawk for 1962. Stevens' illustrious career featured several milestones including the Willys Overland Jeepster and the Luxury Liner bicycle. There were only minor changes to the 1963 Hawk's exterior, and the look was typical of the immediate post–fin era as the fin's influence was drastically reduced. This 1963 Gran Turismo Hawk is finished in Rose Mist and features Studebaker's R2 Supercharged V-8. Studebaker was operating on life support and losing ground to the major carmakers by the early 1960s. Still, the company would produce some fine automobiles until production ceased in 1966.

Signaling the end of the fin era, the 1964 Cadillac was the last to carry Harley Earl's original creation. To be fair there would be a bladed peak on Cadillac's long and straight fenders for several more years, but the traditional fin was now a part of automotive history. What had started with a simple hump on the 1948 Series 62 had grown to unheard-of proportions, and then had quietly withdrawn from the American automobile. This 1964 Fleetwood is finished in Cadillac's pleasant hue of Beacon Blue.

certainly gone, they are not forgotten. A walk around any given car show is bound to turn up a few of the fin warriors from days gone by. Was it just a design concession to the aviation industry, or did it really capture the hearts and minds of a generation? We in the modern millennium are left to ponder this fascinating design aspect of automotive history. There wasn't anything like it previously, and there will never be anything like it again. It was a time when the likes of James

Dean and Marilyn Monroe ruled the drive-in movie screen. It was a time when Elvis and Chuck Berry ruled the airwaves. But most of all, it was a time of some the most fascinating cars that ever rolled out of Detroit. Fins remain an important hallmark in the history of the American automobile. The finned era of the automobile exists not only in the cars that it created, but it lives on in the hearts and minds of a generation of Americans.

INDEX